GOOD MOOD REVOLUTION

MATT O'NEILL

GOOD MOOD REVOLUTION

IGNITING THE POWER OF
CONSCIOUS HAPPINESS

Advantage | Books

Published by Advantage Books, Charleston, South Carolina.
An imprint of Advantage Media.

ADVANTAGE is a registered trademark, and the Advantage colophon is a trademark of Advantage Media Group, Inc.

Printed in the United States of America.

10 9 8 7 6 5 4 3 2 1

ISBN: 979-8-89188-067-2 (Paperback)
ISBN: 979-8-89188-134-1 (Hardcover)
ISBN: 979-8-89188-068-9 (eBook)

Library of Congress Control Number: 2024912628

Cover design by Megan Elger.
Layout design by Ruthie Wood.

This publication is designed to provide accurate and authoritative information in regard to the subject matter covered. It is sold with the understanding that the publisher is not engaged in rendering legal, accounting, or other professional services. If legal advice or other expert assistance is required, the services of a competent professional person should be sought.

Advantage Books is an imprint of Advantage Media Group. Advantage Media helps busy entrepreneurs, CEOs, and leaders write and publish a book to grow their business and become the authority in their field. Advantage authors comprise an exclusive community of industry professionals, idea-makers, and thought leaders. For more information go to **advantagemedia.com**.

To my wife, Katie O'Neill. This book would not exist without your unwavering love and support. I love you always and forever.

To you, the reader. As you brighten up your mood, you light up the world.

CONTENTS

FREE RESOURCES

Accompanying the chapters in this book are exercises that help you conquer your bad moods and live a life of conscious happiness. You can download these resources now at *GoodMoodResources.com.*

INTRODUCTION

What's the secret to lasting happiness?

That's the most important question you could possibly answer. As the Dalai Lama said, "The purpose of our lives is to be happy."[1] And yet, most of us struggle to maintain our happiness on a daily basis.

For me, the pursuit of happiness has been my life's goal. In high school, when asked what I wanted to be when I grew up, my answer was simply, "Happy." Like many, I grew up in a household where bad moods were prevalent. Arguments, upset feelings, and raised voices were common. This is because my father used emotional warfare against us, creating an environment where we didn't feel safe, let alone joyful.

Many of us were raised by parents who, despite their love and best intentions, didn't have the tools or skill set to nurture our happiness effectively. My mom, one of my greatest heroes, did her best with the knowledge she had, but she wasn't formally trained on the science of happiness, nor on the techniques to raise emotionally healthy children. As a result, I grew up seeking answers about how to live happily ever after.

I'm not alone in the pursuit of happiness. To get a glimpse into the mindset of the population, just look at the media we consume. Unfortunately, the news is skewed to the negative to match our negative thought patterns, and the most popular TV shows are high drama and riddled with anxiety. Why? Because that's the way most of us feel inside.

The next time you are out in public, take an intentional moment to look at the faces of people around you. Very few will look genuinely happy. Most look worried, sad, frustrated, or numb. When I stop and notice the look of the people I pass, my heart goes out to them. They try their best to put on a happy face, but the fake smile doesn't quite reach their eyes.

Authentic happiness is not the norm for most people. It's why the most common response to the question, "How are you doing?" is, *"I'm okay," "I'm fine,"* or *"I'm hanging in there."* But this isn't a response I want to have. I no longer want to settle for being *just okay.* When someone asks me how I'm doing, I want to genuinely answer that question with words like *"I feel magnificent!",* or *"I'm feeling wonderful and blessed!",* or *"Today might just be the best day of my life!"* And I want to mean it.

Overtly joyful responses like this are not common in our ho-hum society and most people are shocked when they encounter someone living with incredible joy. It jolts them out of their trance and ignites something powerfully good within them. What we need is more happiness, joy, and enthusiasm in our lives. We need a *Good Mood Revolution.* We are revolting against the norm of blah and okay moods and are creating a movement of conscious happiness.

To live this way requires a path that will lead you to authentic and lasting good moods. Thankfully, that path is here, and it's called *The Progression of Moods.*

The Progression of Moods

In my mid-twenties, after suffering through bad moods long enough, I began reading books about the science of happiness, and I read hundreds of them. I studied psychology, emotional health, spirituality, and self-improvement. In my research, I came across the work of Dr. David Hawkins. He outlined what he calls *The Map of Consciousness*, which is a ladder of emotional states.[2] On this ladder, the most negative emotions are located at the bottom and the most enjoyable emotions are at the top.

Dr. Hawkins's ladder of emotions made a lot of sense to me. I knew if I could learn how to climb it, I would understand how to elevate my moods. But not every emotion on Dr. Hawkins's ladder of emotions aligned with what I knew to be true. Over time, I modified the ladder and created *The Progression of Moods* which is the framework of this book.

The Progression of Moods is the path to conquering bad moods and achieving lasting happiness. Over the past fifteen years, I've invested over half a million dollars in emotional growth to attain these methods. Through them, you will learn how to transcend the eight primary bad moods and enhance the eight primary good moods. Here is the full progression of moods you will ascend as you read this book.

The Eight Primary Good Moods

Peace

Joy

Love

Gratitude

Acceptance

Confidence

Responsibility

Humility

The Eight Primary Bad Moods

Pride

Anger

Desire

Fear

Sadness

Hopelessness

Guilt

Shame

Since creating the *Progression of Moods* framework, I've become one of the world's happiness experts as the host of the *Good Mood Revolution* podcast. I've interviewed hundreds of the world's top authorities on emotional health and happiness, each one enhancing my understanding. At this point, the podcast has been the catalyst for change for thousands of listeners, and this book will do the same for you. It is the culmination of years of research and delivers the best action steps to live a life of conscious happiness.

What to Expect as You Read

In Part 1 of this book, you will learn how to conquer the eight primary bad moods. Part 2 invites you on a journey of choosing the eight primary good moods instead.

To understand how this choice is available to you, it's key to understand the two elements that make up your being. Part of you wants to do what is right and what is good; this is your higher self, or your eternal soul. When you are in alignment with your eternal soul, you are in alignment with the infinite love of God and good moods naturally follow. However, there is another part of you that uses fear, manipulation, and anger to get what it wants. This is the human portion of your being, and it is called the ego. When you are overcome by the ego, you can get lost in bad moods and not understand why.

Part 1 of this book will teach you the eight primary bad moods the ego uses to get you to comply with its wishes. The human ego is not evil, but it is selfish. Its only concern is your survival, and it will manipulate you into bad mood thinking to increase your survival chances. The ego promises future happiness if you do its bidding. But you will learn that happiness doesn't come from listening to the ego. In fact, it's just the opposite. For example, the ego uses *fear* and anxiety to convince you to live on high alert for threats. While this keeps you vigilant in looking out for danger, it also prevents you from feeling peace.

The ego also tells you to use *anger* to manipulate others into giving you what you want. While raising your voice may get you compliance from others, feeling angry is the opposite of feeling happy.

> When you listen to the ego, you harm your joy. To reclaim your happiness, you must become consciously aware of the manipulative thoughts the ego presents you and then decide to let them go.

In the following chapters, you will learn the exact methods to let go of harmful ego-negativity.

Part 2 of this book will teach you alternative thought patterns to replace ego-thinking. You will learn the eight primary good moods that are in alignment with your eternal soul and with God. You will also learn actionable strategies you can implement to prolong your time in these good moods.

Believe me, I understand the frustration that comes from wanting a happier life but feeling at the mercy of bad moods. I know what it's like to be the person behind the fake-happy smile, just trying to hold it all together amidst the demands of a busy life. But I also know what it's like on the other side of this journey. The lessons you will learn in this book will teach you how to conquer your bad moods and live a life of authentic, sustainable happiness. Joy is your birthright and your destiny.

As you embark on this good mood path, do so with an open mind and an open heart. Let each chapter be a step forward on your journey to emotional freedom. If you're ready, let the good mood revolution begin.

PART 1

Conquering Bad Moods

The path to the light of the highest good moods begins in the darkness. At the bottom of *The Progression of Moods* lie your consciousness's most destructive bad moods. Only by facing the emotions of shame, guilt, and hopelessness can you clear them from your subconscious.

We all have dark emotions lingering in our energy systems, and it's time to let them go. Do not fret; the darkness is what allows you to see your light. Without the contrast of the dark, how could you ever see the stars? In the same way, it is only with the contrast of bad moods that you can know the true meaning of joy.

As you read about my personal experiences facing these bad moods, consider how these lessons apply to your life. Think of your own experiences with each mood, and then use the new thought patterns presented as solutions to your challenging emotions. When you encounter an exercise, take out a pen and do the work. Uncovering the happiness that lies beyond the ego only takes a few minutes.

Your life will never be completely free of challenges, but your thoughts can become free of negativity. As spiritual teacher Eckhart Tolle said, "The primary cause of unhappiness is never the situation but your thoughts about it."[3] Negative emotions are not caused by external events but rather your thinking about the events.

In time, you will realize that happiness is a choice of perspective, and each chapter will open your eyes to the perspectives that will produce the highest degree of happiness within you.

CHAPTER 1

Conquering Shame

The Lie of Shame: *I am not enough.*

In 1901, a young couple from Ireland was going through tough times. A potato famine caused hunger and poverty in their nation, and in search of a better life, they sold all their belongings and moved to America with their two sons. Unfortunately, things didn't go as planned. After the move, the mother and eldest son died from tuberculosis, leaving the youngest son, John, to be raised solely by his father on the streets of New York City.

John's father had difficulty finding work to support the two of them. Almost two million people had emigrated from Ireland to the United States because of the famine. John and his father were discriminated against simply because of their Irish accents. They were considered scabs who came to take the jobs of the American people. This created the sting of shame within them, the feeling that they were less than others in society.

The constant discrimination, coupled with the loss of his beloved wife, caused John's father to start drinking heavily to numb the pain.

When he drank, he would take out his pain on his son. As John grew, he innocently believed more lies of shame, thinking he was somehow flawed and not good enough to be loved.

John's life went from bad to worse when his father was killed in an accident at work. This left him an orphan at the age of eight, and his shame grew deeper; he believed he was so flawed that he didn't even deserve to have someone to care for him.

Unbeknownst to John at the time, another child his age was having a similar experience. A small girl in northern Michigan named Marjorie had also lost a parent. Just a few months after Marjorie was born, her father fell ill with tuberculosis and died, leaving Marjorie's young mother a widow with a one-year-old daughter.

In the early 1900s, jobs were hard to come by for women. Marjorie's mother didn't know how she would support herself and her infant daughter. She did what she thought she had to do; she gave Marjorie away to her parents and found a new husband.

Marjorie's mother had five more children with her new husband. All the while, Marjorie was being raised outside the fringes, looking in with longing at the love her half-siblings received from her birth mother. This is how Marjorie also innocently developed a feeling of shame. Like John, she believed she must be flawed and unlovable. Of course, this wasn't true, but these are the conclusions our childhood minds come to when life events are too big to understand.

Time passed, and both children grew up. When John met Marjorie, they were instantly drawn to each other. Emotional signatures work like magnets, and with the like energy of shame in their systems, it was love at first sight. Months after their first hello, John asked Marjorie to marry him, and they went on to have two sons. Life seemed good, but there was just one problem. Because John and

Marjorie believed the lies of shame, thinking they were somehow flawed, they passed these same lies on to their sons.

Marjorie never held her babies because she had never been held. As a result, her sons never knew the tender embrace of a mother. The boys grew up believing they didn't deserve to be loved. Marjorie was doing the best she could as a mom and as a human being. She didn't neglect her babies to harm them; she did it to toughen them up. She didn't want her children to be coddled and soft when she knew the world was harsh.

John, too, was very tough on his boys. John thought he was protecting them from being blindsided when they became adults. Convinced the world would beat his sons down, John decided to beat the world to the punch by beating them down himself. He was hard on the boys, not to harm them, but because he thought it would help them grow up strong.

As a result of their upbringing, the boys developed shame in their systems. They thought something must be wrong with them. A child who isn't loved unconditionally by their parents can innocently conclude that they must be unlovable as they are.

My father was one of those two boys.

The Lies of Shame

Shame is the most destructive bad mood to conquer; it is the feeling that something may be flawed within you. When you believe this lie, you can feel so hurt inside that you hurt others with your words and actions on the outside. But shame is never a truth. The truth is that at your core you are lovable, beautiful, and innocent just as you are.

Because my father didn't believe he was lovable, he didn't offer love or kindness to my siblings or me when we were growing up. He would constantly insult us, tell us we would be failures, and judge everything we did as worthless. I believed him, and this is how I innocently came to believe something was wrong with me too.

The good news is that shame can be healed. Just as I've done with my family line, it can be helpful to trace back the pain of the person who hurt you. Give this a try now. Grab a pen and write out the possible hurt inside of the person who hurt you. When you see how they may have believed they were somehow flawed, you can understand why they tried to make you feel the same way. This understanding can help you reclaim the truth of who you really are.

The truth is you are a child of God. Your very essence is pure love. Your soul, the part of you that lives on after the ego-body dies, is the eternal real you. You are innocent, stainless, and kind. At your core, you are pure goodness. When you separate the light of your soul from the manipulative thoughts of ego-survival thinking, you can heal the wound of shame.

There is nothing wrong with you, and there never has been. Sure, you have made some mistakes—we all have—but your mistakes don't tarnish your essence. Mistakes have negative consequences, and we learn from them. But the mistakes you have made cannot take away from the beauty of the light within you. When you hold on to the idea that something may be flawed within you, you cover yourself in darkness, which darkens the world. But God doesn't want you to dim your light; he needs you to expose the darkness and become a beacon of light for others to follow.

You conquer shame by exposing the lies you innocently believed when you were younger to the light of the truth.

Exposing the Lies You Were Told

I learned how to expose the lies of shame from my good friend, Mathew Micheletti, co-author of *The Inner Work*. Micheletti writes, "Shame stems from the lie that we are rejected, invalid, and beyond the graces of love and forgiveness. It believes itself to be unlovable, unwanted, a waste, and destined for an existence of suffering."[4]

While just about every person has some degree of shame to heal, there is good news: Shame is simply a series of thoughts you innocently believed, and you can un-believe them at any moment. Once you expose the darkness of shame to the truth, it dissolves in the light of your soul.

Let's try this. Recall the individuals from your childhood, such as parents, grandparents, siblings, teachers, or elders, who generated unpleasant feelings within you. Think of those who told you directly or indirectly that you were not enough. Consider the false beliefs you acquired from these influences.

Also, search your past for any experiences that are particularly painful or traumatic. Think of what you may have started to believe about yourself from these painful and traumatic events. What lies did you accidentally associate with yourself from these experiences?

The lies of shame will show up as "I" statements such as "I am bad," "I deserve punishment," or "I am unworthy of love." Everyone has "I" statements, including me. Because of my emotionally abusive father, some of my "I" statements included:

- I am unlovable.

- I am not enough as I am.

- I am wrong.

- I deserve to be judged.

- I deserve to be treated poorly.

- I should be punished.

- I don't deserve love.

- I don't deserve a dad.

- Life is really hard for me.

- I am not one of the lucky ones.

- Something's wrong with me.

Chances are, you have your own list of "I" statements, and I'd encourage you to take a few moments and write them down. There are "notes" pages at the end of this book you can use, or you may find it helpful to download the "Exposing-The-Lies" exercise from *GoodMoodResources.com*.

What are some lies you've believed? Write down the "I" statements that feel disempowering and hurtful. Be completely honest with yourself. Get every shred of harmful thinking out of your subconscious and onto paper where you can work on it and clean it up for good.

Now, look at your list of lies and find compassion for yourself. Imagine telling these things to a beautiful five-year-old child. That's what has happened to most of us. Maybe not in direct words, but definitely from situations and experiences where we didn't feel enough. It's time to turn these lies around and declare the truth of who you are.

Declaring the Truth of Who You Really Are

After writing the lies of shame, you can write the truth of your soul right next to them. You do this by drawing a line down the center of your page and writing a statement of who your soul really is next to each destructive thought of shame. Here is my list of the truths next to the lies of shame I believed about myself:

The Lies I Believed	The Truth About Who I Really Am
I am unlovable.	I am lovable.
I am not enough as I am.	I am good enough.
I am wrong.	I am an innocent child of God.
I deserve to be judged.	I am always given grace by my Creator.
I deserve to be treated poorly.	I deserve to be treated fairly.
I should be punished.	I am forgiven.
I don't deserve love.	I deserve love, and I radiate love.
I don't deserve a dad.	God sent me many strong male role models.
Life is really hard for me.	I've always been guided and supported.
I am not one of the lucky ones.	I am the lucky one.
Something's wrong with me.	There is so much right about me.

Now, it's your turn. Return to that initial list of lies you made and write the truth next to each one. Your list of truths will be some of the most powerful "I am" statements you will ever make. These are the affirmations of your light that you can program into your subconscious. They are the counters to your trauma.

When Shame Shows Up Again

Confronting the lies of shame is an ongoing process. There will be times when you slip back into believing you are unworthy. When this happens, don't worry; ask your subconscious what you are believing about yourself, and then declare the truth.

> Every time you expose the lie, it weakens. Every time you reclaim your truth, you strengthen it.

I've watched this play out in my life as I healed my shame. People used to get angry with me. They used to make me feel terrible about myself. They had no choice. I was asking them to validate the beliefs I had inherited from my father. As a result, I would create conflict and sabotage my relationships. I would do things to upset others, pick fights with loved ones, and create turmoil with my friends. My unhealed shame had me creating proof that I deserved punishment and poor treatment from others, but it was self-inflicted because I didn't believe I was worthy of love.

Once I cleaned up the lies of shame, the world responded to me differently. People started to smile at me wherever I went. I heard compliments in place of criticisms. People were kind to me and went out of their way to be joyful in my presence. I also treated myself with respect and made choices that created harmony in my relationships. Once I transcended the lies of shame, the people in my life validated my internal light and beauty.

This experience taught me that while the bad mood of shame is strong, the truth of who you are is even stronger. Imagine your life when you live fully knowing your goodness. From this point on, you have permission to live in your light, knowing you are lovable and amazing just as you are.

The Lie of Shame: *I am not enough.*
The Truth: *I am more than enough. I am incredible, beautiful, and lovable, just the way I am.*

CHAPTER 2

Conquering Guilt

The Lie of Guilt: *Being hard on myself will push me to improve.*

I stared coldly at my assistant as tears welled in her eyes. She heard how disappointed I was, how she wasn't performing up to my expectations, and something needed to change. By the time I finished telling her all the ways she was falling short, she was full-on crying as she ran out of the conference room.

The tears didn't faze me in the slightest. It was my job to demand performance. My heart was cold. This was just business, and she wasn't doing a good enough job.

As I returned to my office, the front desk receptionist stopped me and said, "I could hear everything you said in there. You were mean to her, and she didn't deserve that."

I wish her words had landed with me that day, but I just shook them off. The truth is that no one was good enough for me. I had impossibly high standards. I found flaws with everyone. People I worked with were never doing enough. I was constantly judging my friends. And my little brother couldn't win my approval because he fell short of how I expected him to live *his* life.

In reality, the people in my life didn't need to improve. I did. Everyone in my life was a mirror for the way I saw myself. I never performed well enough for my own standards; I demanded perfection from myself and continually fell short. I thought my constant judgments were helping. What they were really doing was holding me back.

This is what happens when guilt runs your life.

Guilt Adds Unnecessary Pain to Mistakes

Guilt is the hammer we use to beat ourselves up for our mistakes. We think that being hard on ourselves will push us to improve the next time. That's what I thought, and I prided myself on being my own worst critic. No one was harder on me than I was on myself.

The ego tries to convince us that being hard on ourselves will improve our performance. We think that if we punish ourselves with guilt, we will stop making mistakes. But just the opposite is true. Hurting ourselves with guilt doesn't improve the situation; it just unnecessarily extends the pain we inflict on ourselves and the world.

Every action has a consequence. If you make a mistake, you will experience a negative outcome. Consequences are not punishment; they are simply the result of cause and effect. This is how we learn what to do and what not to do. It is not necessary to punish yourself with guilt beyond a negative consequence to learn to stop making a mistake.

For example, as a child, you were smart enough to learn not to touch a hot stove once you were burned the first time. You didn't need someone punishing you for touching it. The blisters on your hand were lesson enough.

Now that you are an adult, the same principles apply. You don't need to punish yourself for making mistakes. God teaches you through consequences. He doesn't need you to punish yourself further. What he needs is for you to love and accept yourself instead.

If your child were to burn their hand and start screaming in pain, you wouldn't talk down to them; you would rush to them, hold them, and love them. When you make a mistake, you must treat yourself the same way. Rather than belittle yourself, give yourself the love, acceptance, and care you would give to a loved one.

I help myself counteract the ego's tendency for guilt by repeating to myself, *"Even though I am feeling down, I deeply and completely accept myself. I deeply and completely love myself."*

Put your hand on your heart and try repeating this phrase to yourself. The next time you find yourself being critical of your performance, just repeat these words and heal your inner critic.

Guilt Hinders Performance

Guilt doesn't help us improve; it hinders our performance. Because the way we treat ourselves is the way we treat others, we will also falsely believe that being hard on others will improve *their* performance. This is why I thought being hard on my assistant was a positive form of leadership. Like the coach screaming in his players' faces at halftime, this tactic is less effective than positive encouragement.

As three-time Super Bowl–winning coach Bill Walsh said, "People thrive on positive reinforcement. They can take only a certain amount of criticism." So, "don't insult or belittle your people. Instead of getting more out of them, you will get less."[5]

When I examined myself, I realized that I thought my negative feedback was helping me. I thought I was successful in my career *because* I beat myself up for my mistakes. But the opposite was true. I was successful *despite* the guilt I inflicted on myself.

When you use guilt to judge and punish yourself, you are not helping yourself improve; you are only making things worse. Using guilt adds darkness to your psyche, which makes you more likely to repeat your mistakes. When you *feel* bad, you *do* bad.

To prove this to yourself, consider a day you felt bad about yourself. Think of a fight you provoked with someone you love. On that day, the day when you felt guilty about hurting your loved one, how effective were you at your job? If you're like me, on those days, you can't concentrate on work at all. Guilt doesn't help you do better; it makes you worse.

The saying "hurt people hurt people" is popular because it is true. When you feel hurt from self-punishment and guilt, you are more likely to hurt others. The good news is that the opposite of guilty self-punishment helps you perform at your best. When you feel amazing about yourself, you do amazing things in the world, too. When you love, accept, and forgive yourself, you can offer your love, acceptance, and forgiveness to others. This is where performance starts to take off.

Think of a day when you felt incredible about yourself. Picture all the incredible things you can accomplish in these moments. When you feel amazing, your results are amazing.

Count Three Wins Daily

There is a simple daily practice you can adopt to counteract the negativity of guilt and grow your positivity: counting three wins. Each morning, write down three things you did well the day before. They can be simple things at home or work, like making a great meal for your family, completing a challenging workout, or turning in a project to your employer.

When you count the things you are doing well each day, you start to feel incredible about yourself. What you focus on expands. When you count all the ways you are awesome, you will create more awesome ways.

The ego will continue to tell you everything you are doing wrong. It will remind you of the time you said the wrong thing at a meeting, the relational pain you caused your friends, or the time you messed up in front of people you wanted to impress.

What the ego *doesn't* do is remind you of all the things you are doing well each day. To the ego, if something is going well, you have it covered. It doesn't need to waste precious survival energy focusing on it. To help you survive, the ego gets hyper-focused on threats and the mistakes you make. This, it falsely believes, will help you improve your life.

To counteract the ego's negativity, you must consciously choose to focus on the things you do well each day yourself. When you stack your wins, you attract more winning to your life.

I'd encourage you to give this rhythm a try. Think of three things you did well yesterday. They don't have to be big things. They can be little things, like holding the door for a stranger, making a loved one smile, or complimenting a coworker. Write your three wins here:

1. _____

2. _____

3. _____

Counting your wins instantly makes you feel better about yourself. When you recount how you are succeeding, you start to grow your positivity.

To make the habit of counting three wins easier, you can download the Daily-Journal-Sheets at *GoodMoodResources.com*

Counting three wins each day will help you become a much more positive person who has stopped beating yourself up with guilt. In time, you will start to notice what you are doing well *in the moment*. You will also start to notice what *others* around you are doing well. Once I started to count three wins every day, my guilt began to subside. I noticed all that was good about me, so I started noticing all that was good with those around me.

Thankfully, by the time I met my wife, I was affirming all that was right in her. My friends started to enjoy my positivity and encouragement. My coworkers began seeing me as someone who affirmed their strengths. And my brother became a man I respected. Not because *he* changed but because *I* changed. He was always someone who deserved my absolute love and acceptance. I just had to find that for myself first.

When you focus on what is going right, you create more good in the world. As Dr. David Hawkins said, "By changing ourselves, we change the world. As we become more loving on the inside, healing occurs on the outside."[6]

Releasing Guilt from Big Mistakes

Everyone's made big mistakes. We've all harmed people we loved, taken advantage of others for our gain, and hurt others in ways we think are unforgivable. If we don't find self-forgiveness now, the ego will continue punishing us for these big mistakes forever.

To release this guilt, recognize that you have always done the best you could. Now that you are a greater version of yourself, you won't make the same mistake again. But at the time, your choices and your actions were the best you could do. Feeling guilty about something you cannot change is not helping you be a better version of yourself today. It's holding you back from creating good in the world.

If you hurt someone badly, consider that you were most likely feeling hurt inside. And then forgive yourself. I've learned that holding on to guilt for past mistakes doesn't help anyone. Two wrongs don't make a right. As Sharon Salzberg writes, "We need the courage to learn from our past and not live in it."[7]

The only appropriate thing to do when you make a mistake is to apologize sincerely, learn from it, and be better going forward.

To let go of the guilt, fully forgive yourself for all you have done. If you have trouble doing this, ask God for help and remember that he has already forgiven you. The path to being a blessing to the world is full of self-love and self-acceptance. Holding on to guilt is never a positive. God doesn't need you to keep punishing yourself. He needs you to stop holding on to darkness so that you can shine your light as brightly as possible.

The Lie of Guilt: *Being hard on myself will push me to improve.*
The Truth: *Being hard on myself dims my light. To be my best I must focus on all the good I do each day. The more amazing I feel, the more amazing I do in the world.*

CHAPTER 3

Conquering Hopelessness

The Lie of Hopelessness: *Life feels impossibly hard and beyond hope of brighter days.*

Life can be hard.

Burdens weigh so heavily on us that we feel isolated and alone with a mountain of problems. If this happens for long enough, we can eventually feel hopeless. Unlike the destructive bad moods of shame and guilt, the emotion of hopelessness is no longer out to harm anyone else, but this is when we are most vulnerable to harming ourselves.

We all know what it feels like to be completely overwhelmed. Sometimes, it feels like one thing goes wrong after the next, like one giant wave after another. We try to catch our breath, but when we come up for air, another wave crashes, pushing us back down.

We can start to give up on life. We can turn to drugs, alcohol, overeating, and other forms of self-abuse. In extreme cases, we can even consider turning to suicide.

But these choices are *never* the answer.

I write this as someone who has battled hopelessness. At one point, my company had lost money month after month after month. The losses piled up and totaled over $330,000. I was giving all the effort I could, but no matter how hard I tried, we couldn't turn a profit. Then, the next giant wave crashed down when my stepdad lost his battle with cancer. Reeling from the loss and trying to help my mom and my family cope, I didn't even have the chance to come up for air when I received news of the next giant wave. A class-action lawsuit had been filed against realtors that would eventually reduce our already negative income even further.

My future looked completely hopeless, and I felt like a total failure. No matter how hard I tried, it didn't make any difference. I resonated with the words of Angela Duckworth when she wrote, "It isn't suffering that leads to hopelessness. It's suffering you think you can't control."[8] I remember driving home from work and thinking I didn't care if I got into a car crash. It felt appropriate because everything else was crashing around me. This self-destructive thought was my wake-up call. I was no longer just stressed; I had moved beyond stress and into the emotion of hopelessness.

If you ever find yourself having self-destructive thoughts, let them be your wake-up call that you are feeling the normal human emotion of hopelessness. There is nothing wrong with you when you feel this way. It is just one of the eight primary bad moods of the ego, and we all experience it at some point or another. Once you recognize you are feeling hopeless, let these words enter your mind:

No matter how large your losses appear, life is never beyond hope.

Even when you feel abandoned and alone with a mountain of problems, the truth is that God is always by your side, loving you, guiding you, and providing for you.

Grab the Rope

There is a story I like to tell that illustrates the two things you must do to conquer hopelessness.

A man was putting down sandbags to protect his home from a flood that was threatening his town. After setting up the sandbags, he knelt and prayed for help: "God, if the waters rise, please come save me. Amen."

The waters rose over his front porch and his sandbag barrier. Soon, his first floor was covered under a foot of water. He opened his downstairs windows and saw his neighbors getting into a rowboat. They shouted, "Swim to us, and we will take you to safety." Feeling confident that God would protect him, the man replied, "No, you go ahead. I'm going to move my things upstairs to protect them. I'll be okay." They urged him once more and then finally rowed on.

As he moved his possessions upstairs, the waters continued to rise. That's when he opened his second-floor window and saw two guys on a small motorboat. They threw a rope and yelled, "Grab the rope, we'll pull you to safety."

The man shouted back, "I'm good. I've prayed for God to save me. You guys can move on."

The water level reached the second floor, so the man climbed up on the roof. Minutes later, a helicopter came by and dropped down a ladder. The pilot yelled, "Grab the ladder." The man waved him off, shouting, "No, God will save me!"

During the night, the waters rose and swept the man off his roof, and he drowned. After he died, he entered Heaven and came face to face with God. Puzzled, he looked at God and said, "Why didn't you save me?"

"My son," God replied, "I sent you a rowboat, a motorboat, and a helicopter. What more did you want?"

Whenever you feel hopeless, ask for help; God will send it. Then, do your part and grab the rope.

Some Timely Advice

During my battle with hopelessness, I was on a call with my friend Matt Wagner and I asked him for help. I told him I was struggling and feeling stressed. I asked him what I should do. He said, "You should hang around some positive people." At first, I scoffed because this felt like a cut-down. Didn't he know I was *already* a positive person? Besides, I already knew I needed to hang out with positive people.

I then swallowed my pride and recognized that my friend was throwing me a rope. It was my choice to grab it or not. Rather than pretending I already knew this advice, I humbled myself and recognized that I *wasn't* hanging around positive people. I was suffering alone. I took his advice and called my friend Steve Gill, one of the most positive people I know.

Steve told me we always have options, even when situations look hopeless. His advice was to sit down with a blank paper and a pen and start writing out my options. I recognized Steve was throwing me another rope. I went home and started writing down the options I had. Steve's high mood vibrations lifted me, and my plan that day had more optimism and enthusiasm than I had felt in a long time.

My third lifeboat showed up in the form of an invitation to an event with the Sophia Institute, a spiritual community in Charleston, South Carolina, that focuses on mindfulness and well-being. Even though I didn't feel like mingling with people in my state of stress, I recognized that the people at this event would most likely have positive energy.

Sure enough, when I got to the event, my energy started to improve. By the time we left the event, I could feel a shift in my own mood. I could finally feel myself climbing out of the depths of hopelessness. The sun came out again, and I could sense joy, love, and lightheartedness within me once more.

Build Your Lifeboat Team

When you battle hopelessness, I'd encourage you to follow these words from my podcast guest Krista Carpenter: "Don't wait till you're totally burnt out to do the self-care because then you're just trying to do repair work."[9] When you feel down, decide to do things that make you feel good and lift your energy.

Hopelessness is a lie of suffering we tell ourselves when the external world doesn't go our way. When battling hopelessness, I called two friends and attended one event before the darkness lifted. These people were my lifeboat team.

As I learned the hard way, it is best to build your lifeboat team in advance. You never know when you will need them. Ask yourself: *Who in my life can be a positive light for me when I feel overwhelmed, hopeless, or defeated?* List three to five people here:

1. _____

2. _____

3. _____

4. _____

5. _____

Promise yourself right now that you will reach out and ask for help when you feel down. Even when you hit rock bottom, you are not finished. *Harry Potter* creator J. K. Rowling described how hopeless things looked for her as she was "as poor as it is possible to be in modern Britain without being homeless." Her marriage had fallen apart, and she was a single mother trying to make it on her own. She writes, "I'm not going to stand here and tell you that failure is fun. That period of my life is a dark one ... And so rock bottom became the solid foundation on which I rebuilt my life."[10]

> Sometimes, when things look their darkest, only then can we see how bright they could possibly be.

It is only because J.K. Rowling didn't give in to her feelings of hopelessness that we all can benefit from her incredible stories. When things look their darkest in your life just keep going. The light of the day always follows the dark of the night, every single time. No matter how dark things look, just know that brighter days are coming.

Seeking Professional Help

I'm a big proponent of asking for professional help. I've worked with psychologists, psychiatrists, counselors, and life coaches. If you feel professional help can assist you, reach out to a professional and get the help you need.

After Academy Award–winning actress Catherine Zeta-Jones went public with her diagnosis of bipolar II disorder, she was interviewed by *People* magazine. During this exchange, she said, "This is a disorder that affects millions of people, and I am one of them." She went on to say, "If my revelation of having bipolar II has encouraged one person to seek help, then it is worth it. There is no need to suffer silently and there is no shame in seeking help."[11]

Sometimes, we need the help of professionals. If you are struggling and cannot pull yourself out of a rut on your own, get the help you need. There is no shame in asking for help. The only real tragedy is continuing to suffer in silence.

I'm also a huge advocate of prayer. God's line is always open. He listens to every single prayer. You are never alone. Even in your darkest moments, God is there, guiding you. Life is *never* beyond hope, so don't ever give up.

The Lie of Hopelessness: *Life feels impossibly hard and beyond hope of brighter days.*
The Truth: *Life is never beyond hope. When I need help, I must ask for it and then grab the rope when it's thrown my way.*

CHAPTER 4

Conquering Sadness

The Lie of Sadness: *People and positive circumstances in my life are owed to me.*

"Is my baby okay?! Is my baby okay?!"

These screams from my wife pierced the walls of the East Cooper Medical Center and were met with the doctor's eerie silence. Our baby boy was not okay. No cries, no breath. Just a white, limp body as doctors scrambled to save his life.

It had been a long and difficult journey up to this point. Katie and I had started trying for a fourth baby two years before this frantic day. While we understood how fortunate we were to already have three healthy children when many struggled to conceive, we had always envisioned our family with four children. When Katie became pregnant, we were ecstatic. We told our three daughters and we celebrated the good news together.

But at the eight-week ultrasound, we didn't get joyful news. Katie had lost the pregnancy. It was sad for our whole family, especially for

Katie. We mourned the loss of a child we thought we would get to hold and care for.

After some time, we decided to try again. When Katie got a positive pregnancy test, we were thankful and ready to bring a baby into this world. We told our children that Mommy had another baby in her belly, and they shared in our excitement. But when we went to the doctor's office, our hearts were broken yet again when we discovered Katie had lost another baby.

This sadness lasted much longer. We had now suffered two emotionally painful losses and we didn't want to experience these emotions again. It took us a long time before we tried again, and when we did try, Katie became pregnant once more. This time, we were careful with what we shared with our children. Our hearts were still raw.

At the doctor's office for the eight-week ultrasound, we held our breath. The doctor put the ultrasound paddle on Katie's stomach, and we braced for bad news that didn't come. She said, "We've got a heartbeat!" She told us that a heartbeat at eight weeks meant there was a 98 percent chance of a successful delivery. We could breathe again. I cried tears of happiness, and so did Katie. However, we still didn't tell our children. We had been through heartbreak twice before and decided to wait until we were 100 percent sure the baby would make it before we told anyone.

A few weeks later, on a camping trip with our daughters, our whole family made one wish as the sun set over the lake near our campsite. Our five-year-old daughter, Cameron, told us her only wish was for God to give Mommy a baby in her belly. It was such a special wish from such a beautiful little girl, and it felt like a sign from God that this baby was healthy. Katie and I turned to Cameron and her sisters and told them that Cameron's wish had already come true. Mommy was pregnant with a new baby!

Cameron looked at us, and this little angel said, "Daddy, I think God had been waiting to give us this baby, and that's why the other two aren't here." We all agreed with her, and that's what made the heartbreak at the twelve-week ultrasound so much harder to bear. Our doctor looked at us with tears in her eyes and told us that Katie had suffered her third miscarriage.

The Gift of Sadness

Loss can be so hard. As we experience loss, we experience sadness. We wonder why God would want us to experience such sadness. What's the point of it?

While this chapter is focused on the loss of people we love, we can feel sadness anytime we lose something we care about. The loss of a job, of a relationship, of an identity, or of our health can create sadness within us.

We don't want the good things in our lives to change. But the only constant in this world *is* change. The Buddha famously said, "Life is suffering."[12] What he meant was that suffering is inevitable because everything we love will eventually change. We will eventually lose our careers, our relationships, our possessions, our health, and even our identities. As we lose these things we hold dear, we feel sadness. There is no escaping this; loss and sadness are a part of life.

Our path to conquering sadness is to find meaning in loss. If we allow it to, sadness can open our hearts to a greater depth of love. With the heartbreak of each miscarriage, I was awakened to the incredible gift of the children who were in our lives already. I didn't think I had taken them for granted before, but each loss opened my heart and inspired me to love more fiercely than I thought I could.

My eyes finally saw the truth that each moment with my children was a precious gift from God. None of it was owed to me.

This is the gift of sadness. We realize that everything in our lives is temporary by design. In fact, it's only because the things we love are temporary and vulnerable that we can know how special and sacred they truly are. If they lasted forever, we would take them for granted.

Sadness teaches us to stop feeling entitled to having good things in our lives and to choose to feel grateful to God that we've had time with them at all.

The Fourth Pregnancy

Months after the third miscarriage, Katie and I scheduled a visit to a fertility clinic. We were hopeful that doctors could ensure a more successful pregnancy than we had been able to on our own. At the clinic, the doctors did an ultrasound, which is standard procedure before they schedule fertility treatments. However, the treatments were never scheduled because Katie arrived at that appointment already pregnant.

The eight-week visit to the doctor was full of anxious energy. We'd been in that same room with the same ultrasound screen so many times before. The doctor put the ultrasound paddle on Katie's stomach, and we braced for bad news. When we heard the heartbeat, we were relieved but cautious.

On the twelve-week ultrasound visit, Katie and I held our breath. Again, there was a heartbeat, but we remained protective with our hearts. On each visit over the coming months, we heard a positive heartbeat, and we got positive news. The pregnancy went on this way each month until finally the date arrived for Katie to be induced for delivery.

On delivery day we felt light and happy. Katie had done it; this baby had made it to full term! Because Katie had already had three successful deliveries, we had no concerns about complications during this delivery. We were cracking jokes with the nurses as we awaited the moment we would meet our baby boy. I handed Katie a book, and we started to relax as we waited for things to progress.

But then something odd happened on the heart-rate monitor. The steady heartbeat sounded different. Two nurses came in and adjusted the straps on Katie's belly. A few more nurses came in and asked Katie to move into different positions. Moments later, the doctor was there, and then more doctors came in.

A nurse asked me to sit down. She put her hand on my shoulder as a team of doctors frantically worked on Katie. The next moment, a nurse hastily unplugged the wires from the wall and rushed Katie down the hall to emergency surgery. I was left all alone in the room without my wife, without our baby, and there was nothing I could do to help either of them.

At that moment, I saw how powerless I was. The illusion that I was the one in control of my life vanished in an instant. I was humbly struck with the reality that my life was never fully in my hands. That's when I called on the only one who had any power at all. I squeezed my hands and prayed to God with all my might. I asked him to help my wife and our baby. I prayed to our ancestors and all the angels looking over our family to aid us. I prayed with every ounce of my heart and soul.

A nurse came into the room and handed me some scrubs. I quickly put them on, and she brought me down the hall to the operating room. There was Katie on the operating table with a blue sheet covering the lower half of her body where the doctors were working. I went to her, and her face was in pain. There had been no time to fully numb her stomach before the doctor sliced into her belly. I held her face in my hands and told her I was there with her and that I loved her.

Less than a minute later, the doctor said, "The baby's out."

But just as I felt relieved in one moment, this instantaneous wave of despair struck me the next. There was no sound, no crying—just an eerie silence. Katie started to scream, "Is my baby okay?! IS MY BABY OKAY?!"

Silence.

In those agonizing moments, I wondered how we would pick up the pieces from here. I didn't know why this was happening after everything we had been through.

We can plan and act like we have a grip on life. We can do our best to pretend we're in control. But we are not in control. God is. Your life, and the life of everyone you love, is here by the grace of God. Every day you get is his gift to you. We are just blessed to be here, along for the ride, to experience the good with the bad.

The doctor took our son to the operating table and put a mask over his tiny face. He wasn't breathing and his body was limp and white. He pumped air into his lungs. He pumped air again. That's when we heard the faintest little whimper that soon turned into the most wonderful cry I'd ever heard in my life. The entire hospital room erupted in cheers of celebration. Our son's life had been saved by those nurses and doctors and by the grace of God.

This chapter of our lives could have been very dark had the doctors not been able to pump life back into our little boy. It could have been dark had we stayed sad after the first, the second, or the third miscarriages and not continued on with our life in a hopeful way. It could have been dark because life can be dark.

But in every form of adversity, there is a seed of hope. In every challenge, there is a silver lining. In every hardship, there is a lesson. God wastes no experiences. Even the most tragic situations hide shreds of goodness.

I often think that God puts us in humbling circumstances to teach us faith. When things look their darkest, that is when our faith is truly tested. Perhaps we are tested because we are being taught to trust in God rather than in our delusion of control. Or it could be that we are humbled because we have taken our gifts for granted.

I've never loved deeper and with more vigor than I have since the dramatic delivery of our son. It was so raw, and that day gave me a different level of awareness. Life got more real. I had no idea about the level of gratitude I could feel for each person in my life. I hug them more now. I tell them I love them more often. I appreciate the gift of life on a higher level. My emotions have expanded, and I am more in tune with the ups and downs of my own heart.

This is what sadness can do for you. It can awaken you to the precious gift of life.

Evoking Gratitude

Nothing is owed to you. When you lose someone you love, the gift of that loss is an appreciation for life and a deeper understanding of how much you love others. There are people in your life today you can hug. There are people you haven't kept in touch with that you can reconnect with. There are people at work you can notice and appreciate. Today, you can tell your friends and family members that you love them. Do it. Don't wait.

Take a moment to reflect on the special people currently in your life. Think of the people you love most deeply. Write their names here:

_____

_____

_____

_____

_____

Now, pick one of those names that means a great deal to you, and imagine today is their last day here on Earth. Try this exercise with me now. Close your eyes and see what your life looks like as you hear the news of their death. Picture your life as you attend their funeral, and as you try to pick up the pieces after you come home and realize they are gone forever.

With tears in your eyes and your heart torn open by sadness, open your eyes again and rejoice that they are still alive and here with you today. Like Ebenezer Scrooge on Christmas Day, you have just been given the gift of a new, fresh start. You can hug them and tell them how much they mean to you. You can cherish them at a level you have not yet experienced.

I do the above exercise to evoke gratitude any time I notice I have lost it. When I find myself complaining about someone I love dearly, I meditate on the idea that they have been taken to Heaven. When I open my eyes and realize they are still alive, the minor upsets and complaints vanish immediately. I am left with only gratitude that they are still here.

This is the gift of sadness. It can open your heart like nothing else. It can teach you to be grateful for everything you have today. And it can compel you to experience a deep surrender to God.

The Lie of Sadness: *People and positive circumstances in my life are owed to me.*
The Truth: *Nothing is owed to me. My entire life and all the people in it are gifted to me by God. Awakening to this truth can open my heart and fill me with gratitude for the gifts I have today.*

CHAPTER 5

Conquering Fear

The Lie of Fear: *Playing small will keep me safe.*

When my company was small, I had to manage many different departments, including finance and payroll. Not interested in devoting much energy to these financial obligations, I asked my accountant to handle everything for me and mindlessly signed a document that sent him all IRS notices. This felt like a weight off my shoulders—that is, until I discovered he, too, wasn't very interested in this role.

One day I received a call from the IRS and discovered my company had been underpaying payroll taxes for three straight years. My accountant had somehow failed to mention that the IRS had been trying to contact me, and by the time I found out, it was too late to do anything. Years of ignoring this problem meant penalties had been stacked on top of the underpaid tax amounts, leaving me with a $180,000 bill.

I didn't have that kind of money. Not even close. In fact, my little company hadn't made that much profit in all the years we'd been in operation. Further compounding my fears, my wife was pregnant with our first child. I didn't know how I was even going to afford diapers.

My mind went into a tailspin of fear and anxiety. I was sure my company would have to close its doors and we would lose our house. Even if I emptied our life savings, we couldn't pay all the bills. I had nowhere to turn and no way to escape this hole. I didn't know what to do.

This is fear.

Your Mental State Follows Your Physical State

I've had the good fortune to learn the art of overcoming fear from Tony Robbins, the foremost expert on transforming fear into positive action. As a client of Tony's, I worked with one of his top coaches, Steve Gill, for many years.[13] My goal when I began working with Steve was to learn how to effectively conquer my fears. Steve said this always starts with your physical state.

As Steve explained, when we picture someone who is feeling afraid, we typically picture someone who is making themselves small. They have slumped shoulders, their head is down, and they are cowering in a position of protection. When we are afraid, the emotion of fear tells us that making our physical state small is the way to protect ourselves from danger. Our mind makes up all kinds of stories about the scary things that could happen and tells us to hide.

On the other hand, when we picture someone who feels extremely confident, we think of someone standing tall and proud with shoulders back, head up, and chest out. Think of the way Superman or Wonder Woman would stand and move. Harvard researcher Amy Cuddy discovered that when we take on these confident, high-power postures, we begin to feel more confident and less anxious. When we move our body the way Superman would, we increase the confidence hormone (testosterone) in our bloodstream. Standing and moving this way also decreases the fear hormone (cortisol) in our bloodstream.[14] Once we *look* stronger, our minds *think* stronger.

I've found this to be the quickest and most helpful method for conquering fear. When I was facing the IRS bill, I changed my physical state each morning by starting my day with weightlifting and exercise. Exercising naturally moves our body into powerful postures. My morning workouts resulted in my mind feeling more capable of facing the challenges each day.

Now, when I receive a fear-inducing email, I'll immediately put on my shoes and go for a power-walk. I'll purposefully walk tall and strong with my shoulders back and chest out. I'll even imagine myself taking on the posture of Superman. To further enhance my confidence, I'll put in headphones and play a YouTube compilation of motivational speeches. By the end of the walk, my mind always feels more confident and less fearful.

The next time you feel fearful or anxious, give this simple method a try. Rather than allowing your mind to spiral in negativity, put on your shoes and go to the gym, or go for a power-walk. Pull your shoulders back and puff your chest up just slightly higher than you normally would. Perhaps put in some headphones and play uplifting music or motivational speeches. By the time you get back, your mind will feel much stronger and more capable of facing the thing that had created the anxiety.

Ask Your Fear What Needs Your Attention

Fear wants to capture your full attention, alerting you to possible danger. In many ways, this focus of attention can be helpful. Fear doesn't need to be your enemy. It can be your helper if you use the energy it gives you to improve your situation. When confronted with fear, the worst thing you can do is stay stuck in inaction.

Once you make your physical state strong and powerful, the next thing to do is to ask your fear what it wants to show you. It's best to do this with a pen and paper. You want to get the messages of fear out of your head and onto a page where you can formulate a plan. Here are the questions I ask myself when I feel fearful:

- What is this fear asking me to examine more closely?

  _____

- How can I add protection for myself in this situation?

  _____

- What positive actions can I take to improve my current circumstances?

  _____

- What is one step of bravery I can take today in the face of this challenge?

  _____

When I felt fear with the IRS bill, my fear wanted me to examine our household and office finances more closely. This prompted me to cut costs at home and in our business. My fear also wanted me to find ways to get more income to pay off the debt. These messages were helpful; each week, I pulled out a pen and paper and wrote out my plan of action to increase our revenue.

The next time you experience fear or anxiety, ask yourself what your fear wants you to examine. Pull out a pen and answer the above questions using the Notes section in the back of this book. Then take action. Fear's purpose is to inspire you to act. Taking positive action is what ultimately conquers fear.

Use the Energy of Fear to Your Advantage

The emotion of fear creates a great deal of energy in your body. You can use this energy to your advantage once you understand it. If you suddenly found yourself face to face with a tiger in the jungle, your body would get a rush of adrenaline as you moved into fight or flight mode. Your vision would narrow, your heart rate would elevate, and the blood in your body would move toward your limbs to get you ready to move fast. This is a good thing. Fear is readying you to take action.

Olympic athletes are trained to use their fear to help them win events. Their acronym for fear is: *F*eeling *E*xcited *A*nd *R*eady.

The difference between excitement and anxiety is the story you tell yourself about the sensations you feel.

With anxiety, your mind tells you a story of danger or failure. When you feel excitement, your mind tells you a story of future joy or success. The story is made-up either way because you are the one telling it to yourself. When you feel the energy generated by fear in your body, just reframe the story you are telling yourself.

I once heard a college football player say his mantra before a game was, "If I'm not nervous, I'm not ready." He said the nervous feelings proved how much he cared about performing his best to help his team win. If he didn't feel nervous before a game, it would mean he didn't care enough to play his best. This football player had reconditioned his mind to view his pre-game nerves as a sign that he was ready to perform. The same goes for you; you can choose to see the energy of fear as helpful if you reframe what these sensations mean to you.

I used this technique to help my five-year-old daughter, Kelly, overcome her fear of social situations. Kelly was painfully shy and afraid to meet new people. At night, as I tucked her into bed, I spoke with her about reframing her bodily sensations of fear into sensations of excitement. I asked her what she was feeling in her body as she was about to meet new people. She said it felt like she had butterflies in her stomach.

To reframe this feeling of fear into a feeling of excitement, I told her, "God gives you butterflies in your stomach to tell you that something amazing is about to happen. When you feel the butterflies, Kelly, it's God's communication that you are about to have a great time."

Over the next few months, when she was about to back down in fear from a new social situation, I would ask her, "Kelly, what are you feeling?"

She would say, "I'm feeling butterflies in my stomach, Daddy."

"Why does God give you butterflies?"

"To tell me something *amazing* is about to happen."

Soon, Kelly started to get positive confirmation from others as she faced her fears of social anxiety. She realized that when she acted boldly, she was rewarded with positive outcomes. Today, Kelly is outgoing and bold when meeting new friends.

This story isn't just for Kelly, it's also for you and me. God gives us butterflies in our stomach to show us we are on the right track. Butterflies and nervous feelings are a sign we have encountered an opportunity to grow into a higher version of ourselves. Our highest potential always exists just beyond our current comfort zone. The next time you feel butterflies, remember that it's God's signal that something amazing is about to happen if you just act courageously.

Facing Your Fears

Facing your fears takes focus and determination. It also takes effort and action in the face of anxious thoughts. Psychologist Carol Dweck says, "No matter what your ability is, effort is what ignites that ability and turns it into accomplishment."[15]

When it was time for me to do something about the IRS bill, I gathered my staff members and told them we were in financial trouble. I said we didn't have the sales to cover our debt and would go out of business if we didn't work our tails off. Thankfully, those lovely individuals believed in me, and they believed we would succeed. They could have bailed and looked for other jobs that were safer. But the state of confidence I created in the gym each morning before work was so powerful, they could feel we would overcome the long odds and succeed.

We got to work like never before. We arrived early and stayed late. I cut all costs that were not mission-critical, and everyone in my company was on the phone each morning calling potential clients for me to meet. At night, I was out signing new clients while my pregnant wife ate dinner at home alone. We did whatever it took, and it worked.

By the end of the year, we had enough sales to pay off the IRS and then some. In the process, I saved my house and saved my company.

More than that, the IRS challenge had created a power in me that I didn't know existed. I built on the success of our newly elevated level of confidence, and our company grew by 1,500 percent in the next seven years. Our growth was so great that we ended up being named one of the fastest-growing companies in the state of South Carolina.

In the end, the IRS bill that looked like the *worst* possible thing that could have happened ended up being one of the *best* things. I overcame my fears and became a stronger person in the process. This is the true reason you are given fear, to challenge you to rise up and become more. God doesn't give you fear so that you can cower and hide. He gives you fear as an opportunity to *Face Everything And Rise*.

The Lie of Fear: *Playing small will keep me safe.*
The Truth: *The energy created by fear can be used in a powerful, confident way as I **F**ace **E**verything **A**nd **R**ise.*

CHAPTER 6

Conquering Desire

The Lie of Desire: *Manifesting the life of my desires is the pinnacle of happiness.*

Desire is the most complicated emotion on *The Progression of Moods* because it can be used for so much good in your life, but it can also leave you feeling inadequate and empty. When you focus your desire in the direction of your internal and spiritual growth, desire can aid you in becoming the highest possible version of yourself. However, when desire is focused solely on external and material gain, it can leave you feeling unsatisfied and lacking.

I've been stuck in desire in all the wrong ways in my life. I've found myself completely lost in the desire for more success, more money, more power, and more possessions. I would set an insanely high goal for external success, work my tail off for years to accomplish it, and then wait for the happiness I thought would come from the achievement. But the happiness was always fleeting at best. It never lasted more than a few days. Instead, I would immediately compare my success to someone who was achieving even more and recalibrate my goal to something much higher. No matter how much I achieved, it was never enough.

Being lost in desire like this is similar to chasing the horizon. The goalpost keeps moving. You can never accomplish enough, acquire enough, or achieve enough to create lasting fulfillment and happiness. If you are lucky, you wake up from this ego game and realize that desire for external success is insatiable.

I met performance expert Ed Mylett who told a story that epitomizes the downside of desire. Ed said he belonged to a private club that consisted mostly of billionaires. He stated, "Of all the groups of people I've ever spent time with, the club of billionaires is by far the least happy." When I asked Ed why he thought this, he said the billionaires were so focused on accumulating more that they couldn't see they already had enough. This is what can happen if you don't progress your mood beyond the emotion of desire. You can stay trapped in the endless pursuit of more without ever feeling satisfied with what you have or who you are.

The Law of Attraction

Understanding the downsides of desire is important, but so is understanding the positive qualities of this emotion. When used properly, desire can be one of the best forces for helping you become your happiest self. In fact, desire is the first positive step on *The Progression of Moods*. This is because the emotions below desire (shame, guilt, hopelessness, sadness, and fear) have a tendency to pull you back down into negativity. These lower emotions are focused on what went wrong in the past and what could go wrong in the future. With desire, you are focused on *what could go right* in the future. Desire is finally an emotion that helps you yearn for things that excite you and dream of creating a future that inspires you.

Before I formally learned about the positive aspects of desire, I thought that my life was a set of random circumstances. When bad things happened, I just assumed it was bad luck. When good things happened, I assumed I had good luck. Everything changed when I was twenty-five years old and introduced to *Think and Grow Rich* by Napoleon Hill. In the book, Hill states that "the starting point of all achievement is DESIRE."[16] He outlines a three-step formula that will give you everything you want in life. The formula is:

1. Create a clear picture of exactly what you want.

2. Cultivate a *burning desire* for achieving it.

3. Don't stop until you are successful.

Hill's formula changed my life. I stopped focusing on the negatives of my past and put my attention on my truest desires for my future. Around the same time, I was introduced to another resource that helped me cultivate the positive aspects of desire, the movie *The Secret* by Rhonda Byrne. In this movie, I learned about *The Law of Attraction*, which states that you attract to you what you think about most.[17]

Once I learned of The Law of Attraction, I realized that the negative circumstances in my life were most likely attracted to me by my negative thinking. This realization had me analyzing my thoughts on a regular basis. My goal was to remove the negative thoughts and replace them with positive thoughts. This is a milestone epiphany on our journey to good moods. Without this realization, we will continue to subconsciously allow bad mood thought patterns to rule our lives.

After putting The Law of Attraction into practice, my life dramatically improved. The negative circumstances I had experienced reduced significantly as I consciously reduced my negative thinking. Additionally, my focus on positive thinking attracted positive people and events to my life, as if by magic. It was the most pivotal point in my life, and the moment my life shifted from negative to positive.

I became enamored with the power of The Law of Attraction. In an obsessed and unhealthy way, it became my new religion. I started to believe I was manifesting every single situation in my life, good or bad. If something good happened, I believed it was because of my positive thoughts. And if something bad happened, I believed it was because of my negative thoughts.

This is a common trap of The Law of Attraction, and it points to the downsides of this otherwise useful concept. The reality is that The Law of Attraction is not really *law*, it's more of a tool. While our thoughts do attract people and circumstances to our life, and we are much more powerful creators than most of us realize, we are not *the Creator* of everything in our lives. This is why it's important that we continue to progress to authentic good moods. As we progress our moods beyond desire, we learn humility and gratitude to God. With this humility comes the acceptance that sometimes God puts negative situations in our lives to help us grow and become more.

The Positives of Desire

Desire is the pivot point of all positive creation in our lives. This book would not be in your hands if I didn't have a burning desire to create it. We wouldn't be interested in growing our emotional well-being if we didn't have a desire to do so. Desire can be focused and harnessed in a positive way when we set goals that are in alignment with our highest good, and in the highest good of all around us.

According to success author Brian Tracy, "the ability to set goals and make plans for their accomplishment is the 'master skill' of success ... Becoming an expert at goal-setting and goal-achieving is something that you absolutely must do if you wish to fulfill your potential as a human being."[18] I wholeheartedly agree with this statement. You must set goals for your life and take action toward their achievement in order to live to your highest potential. It is only by becoming your highest potential that you actualize your greatest happiness.

I've learned a lot about goal setting from the men's group Gobundance. I had the opportunity to interview the group's CEO, Matt King, about goal setting on the *Good Mood Revolution* podcast. Matt said, "Having a vision for your life and setting goals gives you the ability to create your own destiny."[19] In Gobundance we learn to set goals in different categories of life, not just in our careers or financial lives.

Setting goals in this way allows you to create a balanced and harmonious life. Through my conscious happiness work, I've modified the seven categories of goal setting to give you the best set of categories for creating a life of true happiness. The seven categories are:

1. Health and Fitness

2. Career and Finances

3. Lifestyle and Adventure

4. Family Relationships

5. Friendships

6. Spirituality and Charity

7. Personal and Emotional Growth

Setting goals in each of these seven categories focuses your desire on your internal growth as well as your external growth. By setting goals for your relationships, your spiritual connection, and your emotional growth, you ensure your desire is used for good. It also ensures you won't be swept away by the insatiable nature of desire pointed solely at external success.

Take some time to write down goals for each of the seven categories now. I recommend setting a timer for two minutes per category and writing as many goals as you can think of during that time. You can use the "notes" pages at the end of this book.

Take your goal setting to the next level by download-ing the Goal-Setting-Worksheet at
GoodMoodResources.com

Once you have written goals for each category, pick just one goal that means the most to you in each category. You do this by asking yourself, *"What's the one goal in this area that would make the entire category a win if I were to accomplish it?"* Doing this leaves you with the seven most important goals for the creation of your dream life. This is Step 1 of Napoleon Hill's equation: creating a clear picture of exactly what you want for your life.

Most people fail to identify the life they truly want and settle for living a life others expect of them. When you set goals for the way you want your life to look, you live a life of your design.

Repetition Fuels Your Burning Desire

Step 2 of Napoleon Hill's equation is to cultivate a *burning desire* for achieving your goals. You do this with daily repetition. Brian Tracy notes that, "according to the best research, less than 3 percent of Americans have written goals, and less than 1 percent review and rewrite their goals on a daily basis."[20] It doesn't take a great deal of time to review and rewrite your goals each day. It's such a simple process, and it helps you attract your goals in such a powerful way.

Considering that there are 1,440 minutes in a day, if you devoted less than 1 percent of your daily time (between 5 and 15 minutes a day) to reviewing and rewriting your goals, that would be enough to ensure their manifestation in your life.

Each time you rewrite your goals, you take them from a possibility to a probability. If you write them for enough days in a row, they eventually become an inevitability. Your subconscious brain becomes imbedded with the goals in such a deep way that you take unconscious action to make them your reality. Opportunities that you may not have noticed before start to come out of the woodwork. It seems like magic, but it's just a heightened awareness of what's most important to you.

Daily repetition of your goals is how you grow your wealth, your fitness, and your lifestyle. It's not wrong to set financial goals, health goals, or goals purely for fun. These things are part of living a great life. Just don't make them your everything. Be sure you also put an intense focus on cultivating the most important relationships in your life. Set goals for your marriage, for your family relationships, and for your most important friendships.

Money, fame, and success are the booby prize; they seem so important because most of the world is blinded by their allure. If you are lucky, you realize that the relationships in your life are the true treasure.

Make sure to also point your desire at growing yourself both spiritually and emotionally. Desire a stronger connection with God. And desire your continued ascension up *The Progression of Moods*. Desiring growth in this way will provide you with a life of fulfillment rather than emptiness.

The Lie of Desire: *Manifesting the life of my desires is the pinnacle of happiness.*
The Truth: *Manifesting my desires can become an insatiable trap. I create lasting happiness by focusing my desire on enhancing my relationships, while growing spiritually and emotionally.*

CHAPTER 7

Conquering Anger

The Lie of Anger: *Anger can be used to get what I want.*

Anger can be one of the most destructive forces.

I had a long battle with anger a while ago, and it created much destruction in my life. There was a real estate agent I worked with in my company for over a decade. He had become a dear friend. One day, he approached me and said he was going to start his own company. At the time, I was proud of him for following his heart and wished him success in his new venture.

Months later, he started calling many of the people who worked with my company. After several months, a quarter of our agents left, and many of them joined him. I felt hurt and betrayed. I also felt afraid. As our agents left our company, I watched our income drop into the negative, and I feared the losses would continue. That's when my anger showed up to protect my vulnerable emotions.

The pain I felt was so deep that an angry rage began to overtake me. I wanted to call this guy and cuss him out. I found myself visualizing what I would say to him when I saw him out in public. Usually, these visions ended with us getting into a fistfight. I couldn't help it; I was completely consumed with anger.

The situation I was in with my company was difficult enough, but my anger was perpetuating my suffering. It got to the point where I couldn't even find joy in watching my beautiful young children play. This is the cost of anger.

Why We Use Anger

We use anger to force others to give us what we want. We've learned that our anger can intimidate others and get them to comply with our desires. When we get mad enough with customer service, they give us a discount. When we get angry at our coworkers, they stay out of our way. When we raise our voices with our children, they fall in line.

These results condition us to believe that the fastest way to get what we want is to use anger. But anger has a cost, and its price is always higher than any perceived gain. We don't truly want more compliance from others. What we *really* want is happiness.

When we get mad at customer service to get a discount, we are not happy; we are agitated. When our coworkers stay out of the way, we are not happy; we are disconnected. When we raise our voices at our children, we are not happy; we are disappointed.

The ego's lie is that we can use anger to get what we want. But the thing we want most is what anger destroys. We cannot be both angry and happy at the same time.

Anger Puts Us in *The Box*

Every word spoken in anger must be backed up with more angry words. We do this to justify that our initial anger was valid. Then, we back up our continued anger with more anger to prove our point.

In *Leadership and Self-Deception*, the authors describe that when we are angry with someone, we put ourselves in *the box*. The box is a place where we no longer care about being happy; we only care about justifying our position. In the box, we don't want what is best for us. Instead, we *want* the other person to continue harming us.

The authors explain *the box* in this way: "Whenever we are in *the box*, we have a need that is met by others' poor behavior. And so our boxes encourage more poor behavior in others, even if that behavior makes our lives more difficult."[21] When we are in *the box*, we pretend we want the other person to apologize and make things better. But that's self-deception. If they apologized and started acting nice, we would be proven wrong about their character.

We already told everyone what a jerk they were. We need them to continue acting like a jerk so we can say, "See, I told you he was a jerk, look what he did now!" In *the box*, we would rather be right about our judgments than be proven wrong and have happiness.

Understanding *the box* helped me conquer my anger. I saw that I was speaking poorly about the agent who had left, and I wanted others to agree with me about how awful he was. I realized that I no longer wanted to be happy, I only wanted to prove my point. In fact, I had a secret desire for him to harm me again so I could continue to prove how nasty he was.

To avoid putting yourself in the box, it is crucial to stop communicating when anger arises. It's also important that you don't start recruiting other people to see why your anger is justified. When you find yourself complaining to someone else about a situation that angers you, stop speaking mid-sentence before you box yourself in.

Rather than speak or act in anger, try to bring awareness to your body sensations as you feel anger arising. Get curious. *Where is your anger? What physical sensations do you feel?* For me, it's a tightness in my chest and a feeling of heat rising up my neck and face. I can also feel my hands and voice start to tremble.

This is my signal to stop talking. It's not time for me to type a terse email or send a text message. It's not time to make a phone call. It's time for me to stop communicating before I box myself in.

When I'm my best self, I choose to take a step back from anger-inducing situations. I sleep on them. I don't complain about them to others or try to recruit people to see why I'm right. I just step away and give myself space from the situation that triggered me. This gives me time to process my feelings without saying angry words I'll later regret.

To clarify, I'm not suggesting you suppress your anger or that you ignore it. Suppression will create a whole host of other problems. What I am suggesting is that you learn how to release your anger. Releasing anger is a natural process when you have space to examine the root emotions behind the anger. You release the emotion of anger when you address the core emotions that lie beneath it.

When you feel anger welling up inside, ask yourself: *What emotions are hiding beneath this anger?*

Anger Protects Our Vulnerability

Lurking beneath the surface of our external anger is the raw feeling of vulnerability. To protect our vulnerable hearts, we use anger as a tactic to make ourselves appear stronger. In this way, anger is the second emotion; it's never the first.

Behind the anger is either hurt or fear. The fury of anger comes in to protect us so fast it's hard to recognize these primary emotions. This is why the most powerful thing to do when you feel angry is to acknowledge the truth: *"I'm feeling hurt, and I'm feeling afraid."*

It's not easy to admit when we feel vulnerable and afraid. It can feel much safer to remain angry. But the path to happiness is to set down the weapon of anger and heal our vulnerable emotions. The next time you feel anger coming on, ask yourself these two questions:

Where am I feeling hurt? _____

How do I feel afraid? _____

By focusing on the vulnerable emotions, we avoid the box of anger altogether. We know that anger will cost us our happiness and our peace. To get these treasures, we must go into our anger and see the parts of us we are protecting. We must allow ourselves to touch our wounds.

Getting in Touch with My Vulnerabilities

After months of stewing about the perceived betrayal from my former agent, I finally asked my anger what it was trying to communicate. That's when I got some answers and started the healing.

The first core emotion anger conceals is hurt. When I asked myself, *"Where am I feeling hurt?"* I realized the anger was a cover for how raw my heart felt. I had brought this agent into my inner circle. I cared deeply for him and did everything I could to help him succeed. Each time his office called our agents to recruit them, it felt like a personal attack.

That's when I recognized this hurt was a familiar one. My dad left our family when I was five and subsequently abandoned his duties of being a father. On the sporadic occasions I would see him, he would dish out verbal and emotional abuse. The situation with this agent triggered an unhealed wound in my subconscious.

If I hadn't been harboring this wound, perhaps I wouldn't have felt as hurt by this agent's actions. Maybe I would have recognized that he was just doing his job. Real estate brokers have a job to recruit agents. This was just business, and it wasn't personal. My wound made it feel personal, but the reality is that this agent wasn't attacking me, nor was he trying to harm me.

This is how anger can become our helper. The anger was here to help me heal a childhood wound that was still festering. My work to heal the anger became work to heal the root emotion of shame. I was believing a lie that I deserved abandonment and abuse. I stated the truth, that "*I deserve to be protected and loved*," and I began to notice all the people who stood by my side. There were far more people who chose to stay than who chose to leave. I was being protected and loved every day. As I affirmed the truth, the anger dissipated.

The second core emotion anger conceals is fear. When I asked myself, "*How do I feel afraid?*" I discovered I was afraid that I wasn't leading my company well enough. I was afraid we were no longer a good place to work, and agents would continue to leave. This was an honest fear and a founded one. My leadership had become a bit complacent. I had stopped innovating.

When I faced this fear and rose up, I started to make myself the leader worthy of being followed. I showed up early to work and led powerful trainings. I became a hands-on coach for my team again. I also made changes to pay structures and benefits that helped my agents. As a result, we became a much better company to work for.

This lesson helped me see that anger can be a great helper if you direct it toward improving and healing yourself rather than expressing it toward other people. Rather than putting yourself in the box, ask yourself where you feel hurt and where you feel afraid. Then, take action to heal your wounds and improve your circumstances.

Forgiveness Sets Your Soul Free

The final act of conquering anger is forgiveness. Forgiveness is our offering of love to another and a gift we give ourselves. After spending twenty-seven years wrongfully imprisoned, Nelson Mandela said, "As I walked out the door toward the gate that would lead to my freedom, I knew if I didn't leave my bitterness and hatred behind, I'd still be in prison."[22] When you choose to keep your anger, you keep yourself imprisoned. When you forgive, you set both your souls free.

Whatever we give to another, we also receive. Because of this, giving our full forgiveness is the only reasonable choice. If we harbor bitterness and hatred, our hearts will remain bitter and hateful. But if we give compassion to someone who has hurt us, our hearts will become compassionate.

When someone we care about acts in a cruel way, it hurts. Sometimes, we can't understand why they're being so heartless. When forgiveness is not immediately accessible, we can call on God for help. Here is a prayer I say when I am not able to forgive on my own:

"God, please help me forgive this person. I'm willing to see this situation differently. I'm willing to forgive. Please help me see them with your loving eyes. Amen."

I said this prayer and asked God to help me forgive the agent who had recruited from our company. A few days later while getting ready for work I had a flash of insight. These words came to my mind, *"This agent cannot hurt you; he can only help you. You are the only one who can hurt you.*" I recognized these words as the answer to my prayer. I grabbed a piece of paper and a pen and journaled the ways in which they were true. Through my journaling I saw that this agent was not hurting me; I was hurting myself with my negative story about the situation. My anger was creating pain in my life, and it was hurting my ability to lead my company and my family in a powerful way.

I also saw that this agent was in fact helping me. He was recruiting agents from our firm who did not see our value and who no longer wanted to be with us. By removing the people who did not want to be with us, we were able to give all our support and energy to the people who loved being at our firm.

Finally, I realized that this agent could be a friend in disguise. It was possible that I subconsciously wanted him to create this drama in my life. The drama of the situation allowed me to grow in significant ways, both spiritually and emotionally. I decided that this agent was in fact my friend and that he was conspiring to help me become my best self.

Which story is more true—the story of this agent conspiring to take me down or the story of this agent conspiring to help me become my best? It doesn't matter. Both stories are made up. One story hurt me, and the other story helped me. You are free to choose your story at any moment. Events don't have meaning until you give them meaning. You come to realize that the things that cause you the most pain are your own negative stories. Once a painful event is done, it can no longer touch you; it's in the past.

If you find yourself experiencing pain in the present over a situation that happened a while ago, know that your present pain is self-inflicted by the story you are telling yourself. At any moment, you can choose to let go of your negative story and replace it with a positive one instead. Both stories will be fabricated, and neither will be fully true. To move beyond anger, you must be willing to let go of your need for your negative story to be right. And you must be humble enough to tell yourself a new story where you were wrong about what you initially believed to be true.

In conquering anger, you can either be right, or you can be happy. But you cannot be both at the same time.

The Lie of Anger: *Anger can be used to get what I want.*
The Truth: *Anger destroys what I truly want, which is happiness. To attain happiness, I choose to work on the hurt and fear beneath the anger and move to forgiveness.*

CHAPTER 8

Conquering Pride

The Lie of Pride: *My judgments of others are justified.*

Not long ago, I became consumed with pride, which ultimately put me in a tough situation. My company was having great success, and my income was better than I had ever imagined. Rather than choose the feelings of humble gratitude for these blessings, I began to take pride in my perceived greatness. I developed a feeling of entitlement, falsely believing I deserved better than others because I thought I was somehow better than others.

The house I lived in was nice but wasn't the nicest in the neighborhood. So, I decided to build a big house on the most prestigious street. I found a lovely little home for sale and knocked it down to build a giant house on the lot that would make me proud. For the design, I didn't hire just any architect; I hired the most esteemed architect in town.

The house he designed was stunning, and it was clear to me that this was *the* house that would prove to the world I had made it. The only problem was that I wanted the home to be so big that it pushed the limits of the rules. Neighborhood regulations stated that a structure could be at most 40 percent of the lot area. To appease my prideful desires, my architect said we could bend the rules a little and omit the roof overhangs in our square foot calculations. This way, I could get the big home that would satisfy my big ego.

In my pride, I couldn't see the breaches to my integrity. I justified bending the rules because other homeowners were doing the same. But that's when I got caught by Conor, the town inspector. Conor measured our plans and realized what I was doing. He put a stop work order on our construction and demanded we create new plans that fit the town guidelines.

I was furious with Conor and judged him harshly rather than taking responsibility for the situation. How dare he question me; didn't he know who I was? Why did he need to pick on me when so many others had bent this rule? In my pride, I refused to look at myself and pointed the blame at Conor instead.

Pride Is the Pinnacle of the Ego

Pride is the pinnacle emotion of the ego. To the ego, being on top is the point of life. We know we are feeling prideful when we feel superior to others. This is typically revealed when we judge them, as I was doing with Conor. But pride isn't all bad, and it is a positive step on our *Progression of Moods*. Like many of the bad mood emotions, healthy pride has beneficial qualities.

Pride can help motivate us to achieve greatness. It can encourage us to stand up for ourselves, our beliefs, and the organizations we belong to. Healthy pride can also help us acknowledge our own role in success. This can help us grow our self-esteem and our self-confidence. Compared to the lowest bad moods, elevating our energy frequency to pride is quite an accomplishment. It's much better to feel prideful than it is to feel frozen by fear or incapacitated by hopelessness and depression.

The problems with pride arise when it is overused. Pride can become arrogance as we become blind to our own faults. We can overestimate our role in success and start to feel like we are superior to others. Eventually, this can lead us to feel entitled, believing we are above society's rules.

This is where integrity breaches are justified by the ego. Because we falsely believe we are better than others, we falsely believe the rules don't apply to us. Ultimately, pride comes from a feeling of insecurity.

A prideful person must prove they are better than others because, deep down, they feel insecure.

My pride was covering up my feelings of insecurity. I was so interested in building a big house because I didn't feel big on the inside. I felt I needed to prove my worth to others by showing off my success and my accomplishments.

In our society, pride is everywhere. We grow fixated on posting the perfect images on social media to show everyone that we are worthwhile. We care too much about how our lives compare to the lives of others. We want everyone to see how much fun we have, how great our vacations are, and how perfect our families look in our pictures. This leads us to buy the fanciest cars and live in the nicest houses—even as we crack under the weight of the financial pressure. As Dave Ramsey says, "We buy things we don't need with money we don't have to impress people we don't like."[23]

When overused, pride is a pit of misery we don't even realize we are trapped in. When we act prideful, we are not authentically happy.

The Cost of Pride

Acting in prideful ways can create success; the obsession with being superior to others can push us to high levels of achievement. To the ego, this is a positive. Who doesn't want to be number one? The only problem is that pride has a cost, and the cost is our happiness.

The common saying, *"It feels lonely at the top,"* describes the feeling of the prideful winner. Dominating the competition and stepping on others to get to the top can create a life of isolation rather than connection. You may win, but you may also feel miserable while doing it. To me, external success without internal joy is the ultimate failure.

The other cost of pride is a high potential to compromise integrity. Because we must win at all costs in pride, we can find ourselves bending the rules. We cheat, just a little, to help us win the game. We fudge some numbers on our taxes to put a little more in our bank account. We tell a little white lie that helps us make the sale because everyone else is doing it.

No matter how justified it sounds, breaching our integrity always has a consequence. We get away with nothing. Every action is noticed by our subconscious. When we compromise our morals, our guilty subconscious will find a way to even the score. It may come in the form of an "accident" or self-sabotage. Just know that your subconscious will not allow you to bend the rules without paying for it in some way.

The good news is that there is a positive consequence for every high-integrity decision. When we are honest but lose the game, we grow confidence in our character. When we pay the rightful amount of taxes, we create future financial blessings by eliminating self-sabotage. When we tell the truth to our client but lose the sale, we create a client for life. In our integrity, we may appear to lose in the short run, but we find a future blessed beyond our wildest imaginations.

Our Judgments Show Us Our Pride

If you wish to be free of toxic pride, examine your judgments of others. When you judge someone, you are taking a position of superiority. You think you know better than them, and as you judge, you believe you *are* better than them. But you can never know what is best for someone else. You may think you know how the other person should act, but you don't know the lessons they need to learn for their soul's development. Only God knows that.

As you judge someone else, you pridefully believe you know what the other person is thinking. But you can never know exactly what someone is thinking. The only mind you can honestly know is your own. I learned much about conquering pride from Byron Katie. She created a worksheet called *Judge Your Neighbor* that offers questions to free you from prideful, judgmental thinking. I now use this process to dismantle pride whenever I notice I have a harsh judgment of someone else.

When Conor put a stop work order on our house construction, the whole situation seemed so unfair. Judging his motives, I thought he was picking on me for no good reason. To gain freedom from my pride, I used Byron Katie's work. She recommends you examine your judgments with the following four questions:

1. Is it true?[24]

2. Can I absolutely know that it's true?

3. How do I feel when I think this thought?

4. Who would I be if this thought could no longer exist?[25]

The goal of the first two questions is to shift your mind from prideful "knowing" to a humble acknowledgment that you really don't know anything other than your own thoughts. You may think you know how someone should act, or why they behaved the way they did, but you cannot know those things with absolute certainty. Humbly admitting this starts to quiet down the prideful thinking.

The next two questions help you understand that your suffering over this situation is due to your thoughts, not the other person. When you ask yourself how you feel when you think this thought is true, you start to realize that continuing to hold on to this thought is painful. When you ask yourself who you would be if you could no longer think this thought, you see that you would be free from suffering and happy again if you just let it go. This process gives your subconscious the leverage to drop the harmful thinking and to move on.

In the situation with Conor, I used the four questions to gain freedom from my judgments of him. The first judgment I had was, "*I am angry with Conor because he is harming my family for no good reason.*" Here are my responses to the four questions:

1. Is this true? (Is Conor harming my family for no good reason?) *Yes.*

2. Can I absolutely know that it's true? *No. I can't get inside Conor's head and know whether he has good reasons for doing*

what he is doing or not. He may have excellent reasons that make sense to him, which I don't yet understand.

3. How do I feel when I think this thought? *Like crap. I feel awful when I am ruminating about being harmed. I don't feel like playing with my kids and I don't feel like helping my wife with dinner or chores around the house. I'm so consumed with Conor and this situation that I feel like a shell of my former self.*

4. Who would I be if this thought could no longer exist? *I'd be free! I'd be happy again. I'd play with my kids and be joyful at home. I'd be laughing with my wife, putting on music, and enjoying our evenings. I'd feel on top of the world.*

After using the four questions on this judgment, my mind started to see that Conor was not the cause of my misery; it was my prideful judgments that were creating my suffering. To further drive this understanding home, I used Byron Katie's four questions on another judgmental statement: *"Conor should go to Hell."*

1. Is it true? (Should Conor go to Hell?) *Yes.*

2. Can I absolutely know that it's true? *No. I don't know where Conor should go. That's not up to me, that's up to God.*

3. How do I feel when I think this thought? *I feel awful for my judgments and my hatred. When I get to work, I can't even concentrate. I'm not helping anyone be better because I'm too hurt to be productive myself. I realize that every time I am wishing Conor was in Hell, in that moment, I am the one who is living in Hell. I am damning myself.*

4. Who would I be if this thought could no longer exist? *I would be my best self again. I would get to work and be productive. I*

would inspire my team to do great things in the world. I would spread happiness and joy. I would love my life again!

When I finished questioning the statement about Conor going to Hell, I saw that my judgments of Conor had put me in Hell. This is how judging others works. The situation with Conor was a situation I had to deal with, but I didn't need to suffer with my prideful judgments about him any longer.

Now, it's your turn to end your judgmental thoughts. Think of a person you have judgments about or someone who you feel has disappointed or harmed you in some way. Take yourself back to the hurtful situation and answer the following questions:

• *In this situation, who angers, hurts, or disappoints you and why?*

I am _____ with _____ because _____

      (emotion)   (name)

_____

• *In this situation, what advice would you give this person?*

_____ should/shouldn't _____

(name)

Now, ask yourself Byron Katie's four questions about each of your judgments above.

1. *Is it true?* _____

2. *Can I absolutely know that it's true?* _____

   _____

3. *How do I feel when I think this thought?* _____

   _____

4. *Who would I be if this thought could no longer exist?* _____

_____

At this moment, you are no longer a victim of anything other than your own thoughts. Victims always suffer. When you question your judgments, you take the power back from the ego and choose happier perspectives instead. This is the final step to conquering pride, choosing the first good mood of humility.

You choose humility when you recognize that you become the thing you judge in someone else.

When I was feeling prideful with Conor for harming my family, I was the one harming my family with my ugly mindset. When I was wishing Conor would go to Hell, I was living in a Hell of my own making. Using this process, I finally got to the place where I realized the cost of my prideful judgments was no longer one I was willing to pay.

As Byron Katie writes, "Placing the blame or judgment on someone else leaves you powerless to change your experience; taking responsibility for your beliefs and judgments gives you the power to change them."[26] Your happiness is not in the hands of anyone else; it is always within your power. As you change your thoughts, you change your life.

The Lie of Pride: *My judgments of others are justified.*
The Truth: *Judging others creates suffering within me. As I question my judgments, I gain freedom from my harmful thinking and move myself to happiness.*

PART 2

Choosing Good Moods

Congratulations! You have successfully learned how to conquer the eight primary bad moods. Keep these lessons close to your heart and be sure to revisit them whenever necessary. So long as you are alive, these unpleasant emotions will continue to surface in your life. However, with practice, you will become better at moving on from them quickly. A situation that may have previously ruined your mood for days may only affect you for a few minutes now.

This is good news for your long-term happiness. According to a study conducted by University of Miami psychologists, the longer a person's brain holds on to a negative event, the fewer positive emotions they will experience in the future.[27] The faster you can navigate yourself out of the eight bad mood emotions, the more positive your life will become.

It's important to remember that it's okay to feel down sometimes. Don't be hard on yourself if you find yourself stuck in a bad mood. Treat yourself with the same kindness and understanding you would give to a close friend or family member. Then, come back to the exercises in this book and learn from the emotions you are feeling. They are here to teach you valuable lessons that can help you grow.

This is a new way of being in the world. As you embark on the second half of your revolution, you are not just leaving behind bad moods, you are taking the wisdom you gained from experiencing them with you. It is only by fully facing the negativity of the ego, learning from it, and transcending it that you can embrace a more joyful existence.

As you transition to Part 2, you are shifting from conquering the negative to choosing the positive. This is a move toward the eight primary good moods: humility, responsibility, confidence, acceptance, gratitude, love, joy, and peace. You will find that happiness is not a static state but rather a moment-to-moment choice of perspective.

CHAPTER 9

Choosing Humility

The Lie Keeping Us from Humility:
It's okay to criticize others.

Humility is the foundation of our conscious happiness journey. It is the springboard for all good moods and the antidote to ego. The ego loves to criticize the actions of others. With humility, we see that every criticism we have of someone else is really a criticism of something we don't like within ourselves.

Byron Katie said, "The world is your perception of it. Inside and outside always match—they're reflections of each other. The world is a mirror image of your mind."[28] When we see others as loving and kind, we are looking at our own inner kindness and loving nature. When we see others as rude and cruel, we are looking at our own rudeness and cruelty, projected onto someone else.

Your eyes don't see reality; they only see what your mind *wants* them to see. Eyes don't work like a video camera objectively recording reality and reporting it back to your mind. They work in reverse. Your mind is like a movie projector, and your eyes are the screen. Whatever your mind projects is what your eyes see.

Your mind creates a picture of each person based on your thoughts and beliefs about them. The number one priority for your mind is to be right about what it believes. Therefore, your mind will show your eyes what you already believe to be true about someone, not the full reality of that person. If you believe someone is rude and cruel, your eyes will overlook any kind gestures they make and focus only the ways they are unkind.

As a movie projector, your mind cannot project an image that it doesn't first create. Because everything you see is created from within your mind and projected onto your eyes, your mind must become cruel for your eyes to see an image of cruelty. This is why everyone you see is a mirror into your own thinking.

To see how this is true for you, think of someone you know extremely well, such as a spouse, a sibling, or a parent. Are there days you see them as loving, thoughtful, and caring? Of course there are. And are there also days you see them as thoughtless, careless, and rude? I'm sure you have these days as well. Does their essence change? Or do your thoughts about them change?

At their core, who someone is changes very little day to day. Sure, some days they remember to take out the trash, and other days they are preoccupied with other priorities and forget, but the person is still the same beautiful individual on both days. It is only your perception of them that makes them appear different. If your mind were in a positive place, this person could do something careless or rude, and you would overlook it. On the other hand, if your mind were in a negative place, just about anything this person did would annoy you.

This realization creates tremendous humility. You suddenly realize that your criticisms of others are your path to freedom from suffering.

Your Criticisms Are Your Freedom

Your path to good moods is paved by your criticisms. When you notice yourself mentally criticizing someone for acting mean and ugly, you regain your happiness by recognizing that your mind has become mean and ugly, and then turning it around.

I don't want to dismiss the fact that people do commit harmful acts toward you and others sometimes. But your mind doesn't need to criticize them for doing it. When your mind remains loving, it can notice someone acting in a harmful way and continue to see a beautiful soul who is lost in so much suffering that it is spilling out into the world.

When your mind is loving and compassionate, you remain happy even while dealing with a difficult situation.

This is by no means easy; it takes a great deal of effort to maintain a loving and compassionate mind when others are acting in unkind ways toward us. But the effort is worth it. Keeping your mind in a beautiful state is how you live a life of conscious happiness. Because you are human, your mind will shift to the negative sometimes. As soon as you notice your mind criticizing another, stop and turn the criticism around to see how your mind has become the thing you are criticizing. This turnaround is the final step in *The Work* of Byron Katie.[29]

When you experience the turnaround, it's revolutionary. Your mind stops ruminating and complaining and focuses on healing itself instead. You realize your happiness has nothing to do with others, or how they treat you. Rather, your happiness is completely within your control because it is determined by your choice of perception. Here are some examples of my criticisms and my turnaround statements:

EXAMPLE #1 | RUDE DRIVERS

My criticism when I get cut off while driving: *That person is a jerk.*

Turnaround to myself: *I am being a jerk.*

Come up with an example: *If that driver could hear the way I am talking about them right now, they would certainly think I am a jerk.*

EXAMPLE #2 | BAD EMAILS

My criticism when I receive an email I don't like from Liz: *Liz is such a bitch. She shouldn't email me such snippy remarks.*

Turnaround to myself: *I'm being a bitch.*

Come up with an example: *When I am ruminating about other people over something as silly as an email, I'm acting quite bitchy.*

EXAMPLE #3 | CHEAP CLIENTS

My criticism when a client calls my office to ask for money: *This client is so cheap.*

Turnaround to myself: *I am being cheap.*

Come up with an example: *I don't want to recognize this client feels hurt and betrayed by my firm. I want them to pay us like our other clients who feel we have done a great job, and this thinking makes me cheap.*

By turning each criticism around and seeing how your mind *has become* the exact thing you are criticizing, the ego releases its grip. You stop focusing on the other person. When you turn the focus of your criticism back on your own thinking, you take control of your happiness again. You focus on improving your thinking and behavior, and you become a better person with each criticism examined.

As you grow more loving, understanding, and compassionate toward others, your happiness also grows.

Now, it's your turn. Think of someone who upsets you—someone you have a lot of criticisms about. Write your criticisms down and don't hold back. Then, turn each of the criticisms around to see how your mind has become exactly what it is criticizing in the other.

Your criticism: _____

Turnaround to yourself: _____

Come up with an example: _____

The End of Suffering

If you want to be free of suffering, recognize you cannot be happy while criticizing others at the same time. It takes humility to recognize that all the advice you have for someone else is just advice for yourself. If you want someone else to be kind, what you really want is for your mind to become kind again. The other person's actions are not within your control, but your mind is.

As David Hawkins said, "There is no such thing as a justified resentment. Even if somebody 'did you wrong' you are still free to choose your response and let the resentment go. Once you make this commitment, you begin to experience a different, more benign world as your perceptions evolve."[30] The person you are criticizing is not the problem. Your *criticisms* are the only problem. To choose good moods, it starts with the humility to evolve your perceptions by turning your criticisms around. Make your mind beautiful and kind, and the world you see will become beautiful and kind as well.

The Lie Keeping Us from Humility: *It's okay to criticize others.*
The Truth: *My freedom comes from seeing that what I criticize is what my mind has become. When I turn my criticisms around and focus on improving myself, I regain my happiness.*

CHAPTER 10

Choosing Responsibility

The Lie Keeping Us from
Responsibility: *I feel like a victim.*

One of my favorite hobbies is playing basketball. The downside is that there can be contact in basketball, which can lead to injury.

A few years ago, I started playing with a new group of guys. Because I was the new guy, I wanted to prove my worth. I came in playing with a lot of intensity and the man I was guarding didn't like my aggressive play.

The more physical I played against him, the more irritated he got with me. His agitation reached a breaking point and he decided to teach me a lesson. He intentionally slammed his body into mine and it sent me tumbling to the ground. I put my arm out to brace for impact and felt instant pain in my shoulder.

I went home and iced my wounds, but I could tell something wasn't right. In the following weeks, the shoulder didn't heal, and I stopped going to the court because my left arm was too weak to lift the ball. It hurt so much I couldn't do a single push-up without pain.

Prior to that injury I could do fifty in a row. Eventually, after months of it not getting better, I decided to get an MRI to get some answers.

The results came back with a full tear of the labrum, which is a rim of soft tissue that surrounds the shoulder and keeps it stable. I was devastated, and my doctor said I would most likely continue to experience pain doing normal physical activity until I underwent surgery. He also said that after surgery, my shoulder would probably never be as strong or as stable as it had been before.

I felt so upset about this now permanently disabled shoulder. I could no longer play basketball, I couldn't lift weights, and I even found myself in pain playing with my children. I felt like a victim of a careless decision someone else had made. *Why did he hit me like that?* It wasn't necessary.

The pain in the shoulder was one thing I had to deal with. But the victim thoughts were adding suffering on top of my pain. By taking a victim stance, I was adding a layer of emotional drama to an already hard situation, and this made moving forward much more difficult.

Why We Sometimes Choose to Feel Like a Victim

All of us have experienced times when we have been the victim of someone else's actions. There have been moments when we could not defend ourselves and got hurt by others. I'm sure you've had your share. Perhaps someone physically harmed you, emotionally or sexually abused you, harassed you, stole from you, or unfairly discriminated against you. This isn't right and it's never okay when someone intentionally causes you harm. When this happens, you have every right to feel like a victim.

However, it's important to note that choosing to feel like a victim doesn't help your circumstances. It only adds unnecessary suffering to an already hurtful situation. Someone may have hurt you once in the past, but you can hurt yourself hundreds of times with victim thinking after the incident.

That's certainly what I was doing with my injured shoulder. Every time I thought about that guy hitting me, I got upset. I focused on everything he had taken from me: the game I loved, the ability to sleep pain-free, playing with my kids, and working out. Even though I knew it wasn't helping me move forward, there was some satisfaction I was getting from shifting the blame to him.

There's a reason we fall prey to having a victim mindset. It's because we think, even subconsciously, that we can get something out of it. As we've learned, when we judge others, we get an ego-payoff of being right and proving others wrong. This can lead us to seeking revenge and getting justice, which can feel sweet to the ego.

> The ego-payoff of revenge always comes at the cost of our happiness.

Even if we don't seek revenge, there are other ego-rewards we receive for playing the victim. As we talk about the injustice of our situation and how harmed we've been, we get sympathy and attention from others. We may even find ourselves bonding with them over our pain. As we share the ways we have been harmed, they can share all the ways they have been wronged by others too. This creates a sense of connection.

While there is nothing wrong with sharing our burdens with loved ones, it can become an issue when we do it constantly. Because what we focus on expands, if we continually talk about all our pain, our focus will have us finding *more* pain in life to talk about. If we do this enough, being a victim can become our identity.

Rather than playing the role of a victim, there is a happier and healthier choice. We can set down the small ego-rewards we get from feeling like a victim and enjoy the good life that comes from choosing responsibility instead. In choosing responsibility, you don't have to act like you are responsible for the pain someone else caused you; but you do stop focusing on it.

The past is over, and it is unchangeable. In choosing responsibility, you release the past and focus all your energy on the moment where your true power resides: the present. When you do this, you officially move from victim to victor and reclaim your right to create the brightest future possible.

Can't Hurt Me

One of the best examples of someone transforming their life from victim to victor is David Goggins. In his memoir *Can't Hurt Me*, Goggins describes how, as a child, he was the victim of merciless abuse from his father Trunnis.[31] His father often used the belt to inflict violent beatings for even the smallest things. In one instance, David had an ear infection, and his mother took him to the hospital. She hid it from Trunnis because he would have refused to pay David's medical bills. When they got home, Trunnis beat his mother senseless for spending *his* money. When David tried to stop him, his father beat him too.

The abuse and trauma caused David to develop a stutter. He couldn't concentrate in class, and he fell behind in school. His hair began to fall out and his skin began to develop patches of lost pigment. These are signs of the toxic stress and the results of living in a permanent state of "fight or flight" mode. It's certainly no way to treat an innocent young boy.

When David was eight years old, his mother finally had enough, and she mustered the courage to escape with David and start a new life. However, in his new town, David was abused in a new way: this time in the form of racism. The kids in his new school mercilessly called him dumb and used racial slurs. By fourth grade, he was placed in the special-needs classroom. Just to get by, he started to cheat. By the time he got to high school, he could barely read. Somehow, he fooled his teachers well enough and barely graduated.

After high school, the pain of being a victim was so deep that David gave up on himself. He overate to push his feelings down inside and his weight ballooned to three hundred pounds. Because he didn't believe in himself, he didn't try to get a decent job and took any position that would pay his bills. He ended up working as an overnight exterminator where his routine was to spray dirty kitchens for cockroaches at night. He would then drive through the donut shop the next morning to eat a dozen donuts by himself. As he described it, "I had every excuse in the world to be a loser and used them all."[32] His perpetual victim thoughts kept him further victimizing himself with his choices.

That is until he finally had enough. As Goggins recalls, one night, he entered a dirty restaurant to spray for cockroaches. As he sprayed a nest, thousands of cockroaches swarmed out of the woodwork, pouring over him and the kitchen. That was the moment he decided he wanted more for his life than being a victim.

The next morning, he saw a TV documentary about the Navy SEALs and made it his mission to join them. When he inquired about entering the program, they informed him that he would have to lose one hundred pounds in three months to qualify. He would also have to pass a written test, which wasn't his strong suit. But with this new goal, and a decision to take responsibility for his life, he committed.

He created what he calls the accountability mirror. Each day, he looked at himself in the mirror and took responsibility for the state of his life. He saw that he was the reason he had put on all the weight. It was because of his choices as an adult that he worked in a dead-end job. And it would be because of his new choices that he would go where he wanted to go in life.

To lose weight David woke up every morning before dawn and rode on the exercise bike for two hours. Then, he went to the gym to work out, and then to the pool to swim. He ended each day back on the exercise bike again. This was his routine each day for the next three months. In the off-training time, he studied for the exam. To make the words stick, he rewrote the entire U.S. Navy Diving Manual fourteen times by hand.

With extreme responsibility and sheer determination, David ended up losing the one hundred pounds and passing the exam. After a grueling training program, he eventually achieved his goal and became a SEAL. As David described, "By the time I graduated, I knew that the confidence I'd managed to develop didn't come from a perfect family or God-given talent. It came from personal accountability which brought me self-respect."[33]

David didn't stop there. With an extreme commitment to personal responsibility, he became a world-class athlete. He broke the world record for the most pull-ups completed in a single day with an astonishing 4,030 reps. He also became one of the best endurance athletes in the world, completing over sixty ultramarathons.[34]

David Goggins had every reason to remain a victim. He could have been a statistic and fallen to drugs and alcohol. No one would have blamed him. But he didn't let what happened to him in his past define his future. Yes, he had been abused and treated unfairly as a child. But dwelling on his abuse wouldn't change the past. Instead, he reclaimed his personal power as an adult by taking responsibility for who he was and who he could become.

A New Way to Spell Responsibility

As David Goggins's story teaches, no matter what happens to you in your life, you are responsible for making the most of your circumstances. Having this mindset helps you take ownership and control of your future.

It helps me take responsibility when I spell the word in a new way: *response-ability*. When I stop victim thinking, I can respond to challenging situations in a positive way. The more time I spend feeling like a victim, the more unnecessary suffering I endure.

When we spend our time blaming others for our problems, we are subconsciously waiting for someone else to come and make them right. When we recognize that we are response-able for everything in our present life, we regain the power to make things better. We stop waiting for others to save us and realize we are the only ones responsible for our future.

What I've found is that without the victim narrative, seeing what to do next is easy. For example, if you are unfairly fired from your job, you can spend time feeling like a victim, or you can take response-ability to find a new job. Without the drama in your mind about how unfair the situation is, moving forward and finding a new job is much simpler to do.

If your spouse cheats on you and leaves you for someone else, you can spend your time suffering and feeling betrayed. This can derail your life for years. But the sooner you stop the victim thoughts and take full response-ability for your future life, the sooner you can live that beautiful future. When the drama-thoughts cease, you can start to focus on finding the person who is right for your new future. You may even find that your future marriage is much happier than the one you had.

It can also help you move on when you accept your own responsibility in co-creating a negative situation. Take the example of getting into a car crash. Let's say you get hurt badly, and it wasn't your fault. You can spend your energy suing the person who harmed you and playing the victim for years in court. This will add years of extra suffering to your life as you perpetuate the time you think about the victim drama. Or you can drop the drama and look for the ways that you were at least partially responsible for the situation.

In most cases, you could have done *something* to prevent that car crash. Perhaps you could have been more diligent in looking out for potential threats. Maybe you could have maneuvered your car in a better way. Or perhaps you could have left the house a little earlier so you weren't driving in such a hurry. Ultimately, you can take responsibility for every car crash because you chose to drive your car. When you choose to drive, you assume the responsibility of the risks.

Choosing to see how you are at least partially responsible for challenging situations in your life is one way to end the extra drama of victim thinking. As you practice this, you will become much better at being response-able for creating your best future moving forward.

Living a Life of Responsibility

Ultimately, the happiness you will experience is in direct proportion to the amount of responsibility you are willing to take. With the torn labrum in my shoulder, I stopped playing the victim by looking at my role in the injury. I *was* playing aggressive and physical in that game. This caused my opponent to increase his physicality.

Once I took the victim drama out of the situation, I started to see how I co-created the injury. I stopped blaming the other guy and realized that I was, at least in part, responsible. By dropping my victim story, I stopped the mental pain I'd added on top of my physical pain. This freed my energy to focus on moving forward in a positive direction, and I used this energy to meet with experts. I consulted a trusted physical therapist about her recommendations. I met two orthopedic surgeons for second opinions. I also called my friend Adam Roach who had recovered from injuries and asked his advice.

Adam told me about an athletic trainer he knew who had helped others heal. I hired this trainer and began working on building strength in the muscles around my shoulder, and I did daily exercises for months to help it get better. This added stability to the shoulder joint again. In time, my shoulder healed, and I was able to resume playing basketball and lifting weights again.

Playing the role of the victim is a choice, and so is being responsible. When challenging events happen, recognize that the only one who is response-able for making your life better is you.

The Lie Keeping Us from Responsibility: *I feel like a victim.*
The Truth: *I am response-able for every situation in my life.*

CHAPTER 11

Choosing Confidence

The Lie Keeping Us from Confidence: *I fear I may not be able to perform well enough.*

One of my favorite emotions is the feeling of confidence. I love feeling capable, decisive, and poised. The exciting thing about confidence is that it can be strengthened with practice.

There are times, however, when we lack confidence. When this happens, there is a fear we may not be able to perform up to our expectations. Perhaps we feel ill-prepared. Or maybe we have failed in the past and worry we'll fail again. Whenever we suffer from a lack of confidence, we are visualizing our failings, either consciously or unconsciously. Our mental images create doubt in our abilities to perform well.

On the other hand, when we have confidence about something, we know we can do it. With confidence, our minds visualize us being successful. To help illustrate this point, think back to when you were a freshman in high school. At that time, were you confident you would graduate four years later? If you were like many, you didn't even question if you would because graduating was a foregone conclusion. But think for a moment how big of an accomplishment graduating really was. You had to show up daily and work hard for four straight years. You had to study, pass hundreds of exams, and correctly answer thousands of homework questions.

Even though the task of graduating from high school was enormous, your confidence that you would be successful made the result seem easy.

> When you have confidence, the result feels like an inevitability before you even start.

Everything is always accomplished twice, once in your mind and then in the real world. Whenever you *have* confidence, your mind generates images of you being successful. When you *lack* confidence, your mind generates pictures of you doing poorly. To condition confidence, you must work on your mental imagery. This process is called visualization. If you spend just a few moments each day visualizing the outcomes you most want to achieve in your life, you will drastically improve your confidence.

Your mind doesn't need to know how you will achieve the result. It just needs you to believe you will achieve it. As Napoleon Hill famously said, "Whatever the mind can conceive and believe, it can achieve."[35] You increase your belief by putting in the mental reps of visualization. Just close your eyes for a few moments each day and picture yourself celebrating your goals as if they were already achieved. In time, the mental pictures will become clearer, and your confidence will soar.

In addition to visualization, there are a few other practices that can help you improve your confidence. It starts by keeping promises you make to yourself.

Keep the Promises You Make to Yourself

When you tell yourself you will do something, do it. Each time you follow through on a commitment you make to yourself, you believe in yourself more. When you fail to follow through on a commitment you make to yourself, you believe in yourself less the next time.

This is why you must watch the commitments you make to yourself very carefully. If you tell yourself you will wake up in the morning and go to the gym, go. If you wake up the next morning feeling tired and skip the workout, the next time you tell yourself to go to the gym, you might not believe you'll follow through. Every time you break even the smallest promise to yourself, you weaken your confidence.

Your confidence is like a muscle. With every commitment you keep, your self-belief increases, which improves your confidence. With every commitment you break, your self-belief decreases, which weakens your confidence.

For this reason, you must keep the promises you make to yourself. When you do this with the *small* things like sticking with a morning workout, you start to believe in yourself about *big* things like massive year-end goals. You start to believe that anything you commit to is going to get done.

You get extra confidence points when you keep a difficult commitment. If, for example, you wake up with a massive headache, but you still go to the gym, you have shown yourself that you keep promises even in the face of obstacles. This is important because big goals typically encounter numerous obstacles. Choosing to keep the promises you make to yourself, even in the face of obstacles, creates unstoppable confidence. As you continue this practice, you eventually know that you are the type of person who is willing to do whatever it takes, no matter what. When you act this way, the goals you want are inevitable. This is the mindset of supreme confidence.

Do a Lot of Work in a Short Amount of Time

Another way to grow your confidence is by putting in a lot of work in a short amount of time. When you work hard, you expect to see positive results. Putting in a lot of work helps you create positive mental images of the results you know will come eventually.

Imagine that you decided to work out with intensity at the gym for two hours straight. Now, imagine that you did a two-hour workout every day of the week for three months straight. At the end of these three months, would you expect your fitness to be improved? Of course. You know that putting in this amount of work, with this intensity, for three months would change your physique. In a similar way, if you were to bust your tail at work for months on end, giving every ounce of your focus for ten hours a day, you would expect great things in your career.

> When you put in a great deal of work, you grow confidence in the results you will create.

The reverse is also true. When you slack off and don't give your best effort, you don't expect great results. If you skip all your workouts for three months, you have low confidence in your fitness. If you arrive at work late each day and spend most of your time on social media, you won't expect to have great success in your career.

You can grow your confidence in any area of your life by simply putting in a lot of work in a short amount of time. The harder you work, the more you believe you will succeed.

Make Progress Toward Your Goals

Setting goals is a powerful technique, but confidence doesn't grow simply because you set a goal. In fact, if you set a lot of goals and don't achieve them, this can erode your self-belief. But every time you set a goal and make forward progress, you grow your confidence. Each step forward in a positive direction helps you visualize achieving that goal.

This is why I intentionally make forward progress on my goals on a weekly basis. Each small step helps me visualize the positive results I am trying to achieve. The action doesn't need to be big; it can be simply making one phone call or sending one email. But the key is for me to act on a consistent basis toward accomplishing the goals I've set. Each time I do, my confidence in achieving my goals grows stronger.

I've created a rhythm to help me with this process. Every Monday morning, I review my top seven life goals from the Goal-Setting-Worksheet exercise in chapter 6. I then ask myself two very focused questions:

- What's one thing I can do to help me accomplish my goals this *month*?

- What's one thing I can do to help me accomplish my goals this *week*?

Taking a few minutes to ponder these two questions typically results in two or three action steps I can take in the coming week to move myself forward. Each step increases my confidence that my goals will be accomplished.

If you want to live confidently and achieve your biggest goals, consider asking yourself these two questions and taking small steps of action each week.

Integrity Is the Foundation of Confidence

The final step in growing your confidence is to live a life of integrity. Living of life of integrity means you are honest and fair in all you do and that your words are congruent with your actions. When you perform any action that lacks integrity, perhaps by lying, cheating, or harming another, you lose all confidence. This is because your subconscious notices your integrity breaches and looks for ways to atone for the mistakes. When you do something outside of your integrity, your subconscious keeps the score and guilt is added to your energy system. One way or another, you will compensate for the guilty action and make the score even. Perhaps with self-sabotage, or having "an accident," or by some other form of self-destructive behavior.

For this reason, integrity is the foundation of confidence. When your actions are pure, honest, and for the good of all concerned, your subconscious has a clean slate. You no longer work against yourself. You can only choose *authentic* confidence once you have progressed out of the eight bad moods of the ego and have chosen humility and responsibility. With humility and responsibility, you set down the ego payoffs you get from criticizing and blaming others for your problems. In fact, you stop focusing on others altogether and keep your focus on making yourself the best you can be.

When you act in this way, you create an unshakable internal confidence. This isn't a boastful confidence. It's a quiet confidence. You know your future is blessed because you know your actions are directed solely at self-improvement. If someone harms you, you don't take it personally, and you don't seek revenge. You forgive, turn your criticisms around, and work on improving yourself with the advice you would have given them.

This makes you a peaceful warrior who is doing what is best for your own growth and development. You no longer create guilt by thinking critical thoughts of others, or by trying to harm those who have harmed you in an endless karmic cycle of revenge. The karmic cycle stops with you every time. You grow your integrity, and thus grow your confidence, by living according to the virtues that mean the most to you. It turns out that this approach is also what creates the most happiness in our lives.

In a podcast conversation I had with author Ryan A. Bush, he describes happiness as having three dimensions.[36] The first dimension, he says, is *pain versus pleasure*. The more pleasurable something is, the happier you feel. The second dimension of happiness is *loss versus gain*. The more gain you receive from something, the happier you feel. But this two-dimensional model of happiness is incomplete. You could have pleasure from drugs, and you could gain by stealing from someone. Both actions would be detrimental to your long-term well-being.

This is why Ryan explains there is a third dimension of happiness: *the degree to which you live your life according to your virtues*. The more admirable you feel your actions are, the happier you feel about yourself. The more you deviate from your virtues, the more disappointed you are in yourself. I've noticed this about myself—when I live according to the virtues that mean the most to me, I feel happy with myself. When I don't, I feel bad about myself.

At my real estate company, Matt O'Neill Real Estate, we created virtues for our business, which we call core values. As Jim Collins said in *Good to Great*, "Core values are essential for enduring greatness ... The point is not what core values you have, but that you have core values at all, that you know what they are, that you build them explicitly into the organization, and that you preserve them over time."[37] Collins suggests that you should have no more than five virtues. When you have more than five, it's hard to remember them by heart. When *everything* is important, *nothing* is important. The five virtues for our real estate company are:

- Integrity
- Kindness
- Accountability
- Solutions
- Learning

The happiness of the people in our company follows how closely we uphold these virtues. While we cannot direct the actions of all eighty employees in all individual instances, we have confidence that if they make their decisions with integrity and kindness, they will most likely be happy with their decisions. As a result of living these virtues, Matt O'Neill Real Estate was named the number one company to work for out of 470,000 small businesses in the state of South Carolina. Being kind and integrous in business creates happiness more than any other decisions.

With the success of the culture of our business, I also created virtues with my family. My good friend Mike McCarthy taught me this process and describes it in detail in his book *The Miracle Morning for Parents & Families*.[38] As Mike describes, setting virtues in your home is even more important than at the office. The virtues we instill in our children when they are young will influence their decisions for the rest of their lives.

When I created the O'Neill Virtues, my goal was to give my children five virtues to guide their choices in and out of our home. The five O'Neill Virtues are:

- Be Kind

- Be Brave

- Be Healthy

- Do the Right Thing

- Have Fun

As our family lives these five virtues, we strengthen our confidence in our character. To instill these virtues in our lives, I had an artist draw a picture representing each virtue and hung the framed art on the wall in our dining room. This way we see them and talk about them each night as we have dinner. It is a constant reminder of what we stand for as a family.

Now, it's your turn to create the five virtues that will guide your life. Nothing will improve your confidence more than defining your virtues and choosing to live by them. To help you, I've included the twenty-four virtues created by the founding father of positive psychology, Martin Seligman, below.[39] This list is by no means comprehensive, but it should help you identify five virtues today. Don't overthink this. Your virtues can and will change over time. The important part is to choose five and start the process of living according to virtues that mean something to you.

As you look at this list, which words or phrases strike a chord with you? Which virtues do the people you admire most possess? Circle five from the chart below or write virtues that mean something to you in the spaces below.

Bravery	Creativity	Curiosity	Excellence
Fairness	Forgiveness	Gratitude	Honesty
Hope	Humility	Humor	Judgment
Kindness	Leadership	Love	Love of Learning
Perserverance	Perspective	Prudence	Self-Regulation
Social Intelligence	Spirituality	Teamwork	Zest

Write your five virtues here:

1. _____

2. _____

3. _____

4. _____

5. _____

Defining your virtues is a crucial step to fortifying your confidence. To take your confidence to another level, post your virtues in your home and in your office where you can see them daily. This makes a statement to yourself and the world about what you stand for. It's much harder to break your code when you've displayed it on the wall for all to see.

Confidence is an inside game. It comes from living a life of integrity and by acting according to the virtues that mean the most to you. As you live this way, you will develop unshakable confidence in yourself, knowing that *you* are a person who *you* can count on.

The Lie Keeping Us from Confidence: *I fear I may not be able to perform well enough.*
The Truth: *Confidence comes from keeping the promises I make to myself and by living by the virtues that mean the most to me.*

CHAPTER 12

Choosing Acceptance

The Lie Keeping Us from Acceptance:
My life shouldn't have challenges.

One of the most fascinating people I have ever met is Jane Goodall. Jane is best known for her work studying chimpanzees in the Gombe National Forest in Africa. Her observations were groundbreaking, as she was the first person to witness primates eating meat and to discover that primates were capable of using tools.

In the 1980s, Jane became alarmed by worldwide deforestation and the shrinking of the chimpanzee population.[40] She made it her mission to educate people about the need to care for the environment, and her work as an environmentalist has led her to being described as the "Mother Theresa for the environment."[41]

Jane's work has changed the world, but if it weren't for a major disappointment in her life, she may never have had the opportunity. In my conversation with Jane in September 2023, she told the story about how her earliest life disappointment ended up being the best thing that ever happened to her.

In her childhood, Jane was very bright and considered one of the top students in her class. Her grades would have easily qualified her to attend the University of Cambridge, which is where she wanted to go. However, her family didn't have the financial means for Jane to attend university. Instead, she needed to get a job to help with family living expenses.

Jane dutifully worked as a secretary, forgoing her heart's desire to attend college. She disliked the job; it was menial and undermined her talents and intellect. She felt disappointed with where her life was going, but little did she know that God had plans for her that she couldn't see. Everything was working out exactly as it should for reasons that didn't make sense at the time.

After working for years as a secretary, one of Jane's friends invited her on a trip to Africa. Jane jumped at the opportunity. To afford the trip, she took on a second job as a waitress and saved every penny. Then, in 1957, she boarded a ship and made her way to Nairobi, Kenya.[42] While there, Jane was introduced to an archaeologist named Dr. Louis Leakey. Coincidentally, Mr. Leakey's secretary had quit just a few weeks before Jane's trip, and he was looking for a replacement.

That's when Jane's biggest disappointment became her biggest advantage. Her menial secretary job helped her secure a job with Dr. Leakey and allowed her to stay in Africa studying the animals. It was only because of her earlier disappointment that she was able to fulfill her destiny.

Sometimes, what appears to be a setback is really a setup for something extraordinary in our lives.

In Jane's case, God knew exactly what he was doing when he nudged her toward the secretary training. If Jane could have trusted that her secretary experience was exactly what was going to be best in the long run, she wouldn't have needed to feel any disappointment. In fact, she may have even found herself feeling grateful for the experience.

What Initially Appears Negative Will Make Sense in Time

When we choose the good mood of acceptance, we choose to trust in God. We know that events that may initially appear negative will make sense in time—sometimes, only after this lifetime. As we sharpen our acceptance, we begin to accept every event, good or bad, as if it were a gift sent from God to help us.

Sometimes, it's hard to see how something could be a blessing in disguise. But any life experience, no matter how negative it may seem initially, can bring benefits if we choose to look for them. With time, it will become apparent that everything that happens is a necessary part of our story. If we look hard enough for long enough, we can find the silver lining.

As we embrace the emotion of acceptance, we stop judging our experience in the moment. We choose to enthusiastically accept all events in our lives. We come to know that our happiness is enhanced by our ability to see how everything is supporting our highest good in the long run. One of my favorite stories about acceptance is from the book *The Compound Effect*.[43] This is my adaptation of that story.

On a farm outside of town, there lived a wise old farmer and his son. One late summer evening, a storm came through and damaged the fencing to the horse pastures, causing all the horses to run off. The farmer's neighbors came by and told the farmer they were sorry for his misfortune. The wise old farmer said, "This could be good, but only time will tell."

That afternoon the farmer and his son went out to find the horses. When they caught up to them, they noticed they had joined a herd of wild horses. The farmer was able to rope in his horses, as well as an impressive wild stallion. When they got back to the farm, the neighbors came by and congratulated the farmer for his good fortune. The farmer said, "This could be good, but only time will tell."

Back at the farm, the son tried to break the wild stallion. It bucked him so hard that he fell off and broke his leg. The neighbors came by to console the farmer for misfortune. He simply said, "This could be good, but only time will tell."

Later that month, the military came through town to take all able-bodied young men to war. The farmer's son was spared because of his injured leg. The neighbors all rejoiced. The wise old farmer said, "This could be good, but only time will tell."

This story could go on and on with the wise old farmer holding back any negative judgments of external events as they happen. I think of this story often as a reminder that I can never know if a disappointment is really a setup for a future blessing. We can all become more like the farmer and accept that things will eventually make sense down the road. We have each experienced events that initially felt like major setbacks. It is only with the gift of time that we can look back on such events and see the gifts they brought us.

Living Without Regrets

As we embody acceptance, we choose to live a life without regrets. People often ask, "If you could change one thing about your past, what would it be?" My answer is always the same: "I would change nothing."

Everything that has ever happened was necessary to get me to this exact moment today. I am so thrilled with what my life is now that I would take none of it back. Even one small change might have sent my entire life in a completely different direction, and I don't want to be anywhere other than where I am right now.

I am so grateful for the lessons I have learned and the insights I have gained. Some events were painful to live through. And while I wouldn't want to experience them again, I also wouldn't take them back. I have gained valuable knowledge and understanding from each situation.

As a young boy, the emotional abuse I endured from my father is the reason I became so interested in learning how to heal. It's also the reason I committed my life to spreading joy. My pain became my purpose. I made it my mission to help others heal so they would stop adding suffering to the world, and instead add joy and love to others.

With acceptance, you see that God wastes no experiences. Even the most challenging experience can enrich your soul with profound wisdom, compassion, and understanding.

> When your heart breaks, it doesn't shatter; it breaks
> open. In those moments, take time to look at the
> treasures inside before you patch it back up. Each
> disappointment is here for your growth.

Connecting the Dots

With acceptance, you develop a fierce trust in God. You trust that whatever events and circumstances God gives you will be for your highest good in the long run. As you strengthen this incredible emotion, you begin to accept challenging events *as they happen*. You know that while they may *appear* negative, they will eventually make sense. In some cases, the full meaning of the event will only become apparent after this lifetime, but in all cases, you can trust that absolutely everything is being guided by God's infinite love for you.

This is the path of conscious happiness. You see that your mood is not caused by the events or conditions in your life but rather by your choice of perspective. In his famous commencement speech to Stanford, Steve Jobs described how the events in our lives always seem to make sense in time. He said,

> "If I had never dropped out, I would have never dropped in on this calligraphy class, and personal computers might not have the wonderful typography that they do. Of course it was impossible to connect the dots looking forward when I was in college. But it was very, very clear looking backward ten years later ... you can't connect the dots looking forward; you can only connect them looking backward. So, you have to trust that the dots will somehow connect in your future."[44]

To help you connect the dots looking forward and thus develop your acceptance, there is an exercise that was taught to me by my friend Mathew Micheletti, co-author of *The Inner Work*. This exercise has you consider challenging events, and then think about the positives they created in your life. Here's an example of this excercise from my life.

Example: Challenging Experience: <u>My stepfather lost his battle with cancer.</u>

- What did you learn? <u>That life is precious, and that no one I love is guaranteed to be here tomorrow. I must appreciate and love them fully today.</u>

- How did you grow? <u>I became more openly loving to those who matter in my life.</u>

- How did this experience forge you into a greater version of yourself? <u>I became a protector for my mom in a whole new way. My responsibility for her grew to levels I didn't know it could.</u>

Now it's your turn. Think back on a few challenging times in your life. Write them down here and answer the following questions:

1. Challenging Experience 1: _____

   - What did you learn? _____
   _____

   - How did you grow? _____
   _____

   - How did this experience forge you into a greater version of yourself? _____
   _____

2. Challenging Experience 2: _____

   - What did you learn? _____
   _____

   - How did you grow? _____
   _____

   - How did this experience forge you into a greater version of yourself? _____
   _____

3. Challenging Experience 3: _____

   - What did you learn? _____
   _____

   - How did you grow? _____
   _____

   - How did this experience forge you into a greater version of yourself? _____
   _____

Thinking back on challenging moments in your life and connecting the dots forward allows you to see how your experiences helped you become who you are today. This empowers you to trust that the dots will also connect in your future.

The Forging Process

A blacksmith forges a piece of iron by throwing it into the fire and then beating it with a large hammer. This intense trauma turns raw iron into something more useful and beautiful. In the same way, your challenging experiences forge you into a more useful and beautiful version of yourself.

Connecting the dots helps you understand that the forging process *is the blessing*. Without your adversities, you wouldn't be who you are today. Like Jane Goodall, you may even notice that your life's biggest disappointments were what you needed most to fulfill your destiny.

As you move forward, you will continue to encounter challenging experiences. You can resist, complain, and get bent out of shape about them. Or you can accept them and choose to have gratitude *as you experience challenges*. You do this by accepting that each challenge is here to forge you into a greater version of yourself. While the forging process is not comfortable, you begin to know that it will ultimately shape you into who you are meant to become.

The Lie Keeping Us from Acceptance: *My life shouldn't have challenges.*
The Truth: *Every challenge is a gift to help me grow. I can trust that given a long enough timeline, it will all make sense.*

CHAPTER 13

Choosing Gratitude

The Lie Keeping Us from Gratitude:
There isn't much to feel grateful for.

I wake up some mornings and don't feel very grateful. Sometimes, my mind is racing with all the to-dos and stresses of life. For this reason, I consciously start my mornings by choosing gratitude, whether I feel like it or not.

As I get out of bed and put my first foot on the floor, I say, *"Thank."* Then, as my other foot hits the floor, I say, *"You."* With each successive step, I quietly repeat, "Thank you, thank you, thank you."

If you repeat the words *"thank you"* to start each day, especially on the mornings when you don't feel like it, you too will strengthen your gratitude. There is a very good reason to do this—*Gratitude is the gateway to good moods*. It's not always possible to go from a bad mood to immediately feeling happy. But it *is* possible to go from a bad mood to feeling grateful for being alive. Then, once you are grateful, you can shift back into a good mood.

When your heart is full of gratitude, you stop focusing on what's wrong. You no longer see what is bad or lacking. Rather, with gratitude, you know that in this very moment, you have absolutely everything you need. In fact, if you think about it, all your needs have *always* been met. Can you think of a single moment when you haven't had what you needed to survive? No, that's impossible. If you weren't given what you needed to survive, you wouldn't be here to read these words.

For this reason, you can say, *"Thank you, God, for giving me what I need today."* Because of him, you have enough air to breathe, water to drink, and food to eat to sustain your existence. What a blessing. You are supported in countless ways by countless forces. The sun provides you with warmth. The soil provides nutrients for your food to grow. The chair you sit on supports your body. The shelter you are in protects you from the weather. By getting present to notice all that supports you, you can feel overwhelming gratitude for all your blessings.

Life Can Be a Picnic

God blesses you when you are grateful. He also blesses you when you are not grateful, but you just don't notice it. Several years ago, I was attending a Tony Robbins event where he shared this powerful story. He described two people having a conversation with God while on a picnic. One was grateful, and one was not. The ungrateful person complained to God and said,

> God, why did you make it so hot here? I'm sweating. It's uncomfortable. If you're the master of the universe, couldn't you just make it seventy-five degrees all the time? And even when I move into the shade to cool down, it's still miserable here. These damn mosquitoes bite me and suck my blood. Why did you have to make these bloodsuckers? And look at that tree, it's all bent and

crooked. It looks terrible. Couldn't you make trees that look right? And now look, even more trouble. The clouds are turning dark, and it's starting to rain. This picnic is ruined! Why did I even bother?

The other person at the park that day was the grateful person. With a heart full of gratitude, their conversation with God sounded quite different. They said:

God, thank you for this beautiful day! I love it when the sun is out because it just makes me so happy. I don't know how you did it, but you suspended a giant ball of fire in the middle of space just to keep us warm. That's really remarkable. You also created trees to give me shade; I love sitting in the shade on a nice summer day. Also, thank you for creating these little mosquitoes, they teach me so much about life. They are so tiny, and yet, they have the audacity to come and bite me, a giant. They inspire me to be brave and to take on the giants in my life. And I just love all the variety in the life you have created. Just look at the beautiful, crooked tree. It's so cool the way it continues to grow and thrive in spite of being broken; it reminds me of my own resilience. And now look at this! You are always thinking, God, you brought an afternoon shower to cool me down. I just love sitting in the pavilion and watching the rain. It's the perfect day. Thank you, God!"

Which of these two people do you think God would be more likely to bless—the one who complains about all the gifts received or the one who expresses gratitude for them? Who would you rather spend time with between the two? Who would you rather be today? The truth is that we are capable of being *both* people. Whatever we look for, we will find. Decide to spend your time looking for things to be grateful for, and your happiness will improve.

Today's Problems Were Your Dreams Years Ago

Most of the things I complain about today are what I wished for earlier in my life. Sometimes, I complain about how hard my job is. In these moments, I forget that this was the job I wished for just a few years ago.

Sometimes, when I feel tired, I complain about my kids. I get upset about them not listening, not helping, and acting wild when I wish they would behave. In these moments, I forget that these were the same children I prayed to have one day.

I complain that my body is injured. I feel frustrated my leg is sore, or I have a pulled muscle. But I forget that I always wished I would still be alive with a body that could remain athletic and active in my forties.

What do you complain about? Do you complain about your coworkers? Do you complain about your spouse? Do you gripe about technology?

If so, it can be helpful to remember that each of these was once a dream. Your current job was once a job you wished you could have. Your spouse was once a person you hoped would date you. The technology you are upset with was once thought unimaginable. The next time you catch yourself complaining, pause and see if this "problem" was once a dream you wished you could have.

Turn Your "Have-Tos" into "Get-Tos"

Last year, I was ungrateful at my office. The refrigerator handle was loose, and it annoyed me that no one fixed it. Every time I reached for it, I felt frustrated that it was still broken. I kept waiting for one of the staff members, who also used the refrigerator, to call a handyman and have it repaired.

After months of it being loose, one day, I went to open the refrigerator, and the handle came right off the door. I felt so frustrated that no one cared enough to make this right. I also felt overwhelmed that so many things fell on my shoulders. Couldn't someone who was not the CEO have a refrigerator door fixed?

The next day, I brought in tools from home, feeling a strong lack of gratitude. As I lay on my back on the kitchen floor, a thought occurred that snapped me out of my funk. I decided to turn my *"have-tos"* into *"get-tos."*

I didn't *have-to* fix the refrigerator door. I *got* the opportunity to fix it. I thought, "I *get-to* fix this refrigerator because I am fortunate enough to have a refrigerator to fix. Just two hundred years ago, not a single person in the world had an electric refrigerator. How lucky am I that I have this machine that keeps my lunch cold and ready for me each day?"

I thought, "I *get-to* fix this door because I have hands that allow me to. Some people, like my podcast guest Wendy Wallace, don't have hands. I'm sure Wendy would be so happy to use her hands to fix something that was broken.

"I also *get-to* fix this door because I am alive today and can fix it. Not everyone woke up alive this morning. Over a hundred thousand people died yesterday, and they don't have the opportunity to fix things in their lives today, but I do."

This thought process allowed me to switch from being annoyed with my coworkers to grateful. I thought, "I *get-to* fix this door today because I have a chance to send love to my entire company, caring for them and supporting them. Perhaps a secure door handle will make someone feel more secure in their career today. I *get-to* be of service today. Not everyone gets to be of service, and many would trade places with me in a heartbeat."

The next time you feel ungrateful, make this switch. When you catch yourself complaining about the things you *have-to* do, remember that you can easily flip back into gratitude by counting all the ways you *get-to* do the things you are doing.

Prayers of Gratitude

Gratitude doesn't come naturally to any of us, and it's non-existent when we are caught up in the ego. To the ego, gratitude is a waste of time. Taking time to think about what we are grateful for doesn't help the ego in the slightest with survival. But the E.G.O. is an acronym for Edging God Out. The ego is so self-centered it fails to acknowledge a higher power or give credit to anyone or anything other than itself.

When you are feeling ungrateful, you are listening to the ego. However, when you are feeling grateful, you must be grateful *to something*. That something is a higher power. It could be your gratitude to the universe. For me, it's gratitude to God for creating and sustaining my life.

To foster my gratitude, I use prayer. Each morning, I put my hand on my heart and wait until I can feel my heart beating. I breathe into my chest and experience what it feels like to be alive. This gets me out of my head, where the ego lives, and aligned with my body, which is in touch with the eternal present moment. God doesn't exist in the mind; God exists in the only real time we can ever experience, which is the present. As I feel my heart beating in my hands, I get a rush of the magnificent feeling of being alive today. I notice that I have an opportunity to live this day because God has willed it.

From this place of presence, I say a prayer of gratitude to God. I say, "Dear God, thank you for this heartbeat. Thank you for today. Thank you for yesterday and for each of the things that happened" (I call them out, one by one). Then, I pray for God to guide me on this day, saying, "God, guide me today. Guide my thoughts and actions. Guide my heart and my mind during each encounter today [listed out, one by one]. Let me do and say the things that will best serve all concerned. Amen."

Starting my morning with humble prayers of gratitude is one of my best routines. I used to think God was too busy to help me every day. I figured I would only call on him when I needed him, but I've since learned that God is not like me and doesn't have a limit to his attention.

God is so powerful he can help everyone with everything simultaneously. In fact, he *wants* to help with everything. But he will only help when invited by prayer. Otherwise, he would be encroaching on your free will, which he will not do. If you prefer to solve everything on your own, he will allow you to struggle. Your free will is God's ultimate gift to you, and he will not take it back.

I prefer to appreciate my free will, while also asking for daily guidance. I see prayer as my daily appointment with God. And during every appointment I have with him, I make sure to express my gratitude.

Write Three New Gratitudes Each Day

The gratitude routine I have been practicing the longest is to write down things I am grateful for. After I pray, I grab my journal and ask myself, "What are three new things I am grateful for today?"

I don't repeat the same three things each day because that would become boring and make gratitude feel like a chore. To keep gratitude fresh and exciting, I search my brain for three brand-new things I am grateful for each day. Thinking of these new things is the secret ingredient to finding gratitude for everything in life. After a few months of this practice, you eventually run out of things to be grateful for. You will have already mentioned your spouse, each of your kids, your job, all your coworkers, and your dog. So, what else is there?

At this point, you start to find ways to be grateful for every experience from the day before. You think of the workout you did, the flower you saw on your walk, the smile of the person you saw in the checkout line, and the problem you had that led to an insight. By forcing yourself to think of three new things each day, you realize you can feel gratitude for every experience in your life.

If you get hit in the mouth and need stitches, you can be grateful for the doctors who stitch you up rather than feeling upset about the situation. If you get into an accident on your way to work, you can be grateful you are safe rather than focusing on the damage done to your car. If you lose money in a business deal, you can be grateful for the lessons rather than ruminate over the losses.

When you create a habit of writing down three new things each morning, your brain will keep an open gratitude file. It will stay vigilant, counting your blessings as they occur to help you write them down the next morning. This practice helps you feel grateful as you experience your life each moment.

Now, it's your turn. Think of three new things you are grateful for and write them here:

1. _____

2. _____

3. _____

Do this practice again tomorrow. Counting three things you are grateful for each day will improve your happiness. It takes only a few moments, and it will help you feel blessed instead of stressed.

You cannot overdo gratitude. When you commit to becoming more grateful each day, you naturally become happier. Gratitude is the gateway emotion to the highest good moods. It's not always possible to go from a bad mood to a joyful one, but it is possible to go from a bad mood to a grateful one. From that place of gratitude, you can access the highest good moods of all: Love, Joy, and Peace.

The Lie Keeping Us from Gratitude: *There isn't much to feel grateful for.*
The Truth: *Gratitude is a choice, and it gets stronger with practice. When I choose to practice gratitude each day, my happiness naturally follows.*

C H A P T E R 1 4

Choosing Love

The Lie Keeping Us from Love: *I don't feel like being loving.*

One summer my family and I visited my good friend Avi in Washington, D.C. It was the Fourth of July, and I wanted to keep the kids up late to see the fireworks. Katie wanted to put our children to bed early so they would be fresh for sightseeing the next morning.

I postured hard to stay up late. We were in our nation's capital, and I was sure the fireworks show would be a lifelong memory for our family. I used every tactic I could to convince Katie this was a good idea. But she held her ground. She was convinced the children would turn into a hot mess and we would have a miserable experience.

I finally relented, but I didn't do so without letting Katie know I was displeased with the outcome. The entire drive back to the hotel, I was stewing at not getting my way. In that moment, I subconsciously closed my heart toward Katie and used my coldness as a tool of manipulation.

By the time we got back to the hotel, I was in a full-blown bad mood. Not because of Katie and her decision to skip the fireworks. My bad mood was self-created by my loveless thinking; I had failed to choose love. Instead, I completely shut down all happiness and was cold and standoffish.

Katie retaliated with her own icy coldness toward me. She wasn't saying a word. She wouldn't even look at me as we passed each other in the hotel room. Had I made a different choice, to keep my heart open to Katie, I could have driven us home in a joyful way. I could have tucked my children into their beds and playfully read bedtime stories. Then, I could have passionately kissed my wife and continued to live in happiness.

The important point is that any time you close your heart, you lose, whether it gets you the result you want or not. Closing your heart creates suffering in you and in the other person. This is a lose-lose situation. No external gain is worth the cost of your love and happiness.

A World Guided by Love

When we perceive reality correctly, we perceive a world guided by the perfect love of God. The *Progression of Moods* is a progression toward this ultimate understanding.

Conquering the eight primary bad moods clears up our misperceptions of reality that shield our hearts from feeling love.

> As we begin to consciously choose good moods, we realize that our happiness is not due to what others said or did, or what happened or didn't happen. We come to know that our happiness is our choice of perception.

This brings us to a very important question: *Which choice of perception gives us the most happiness in our hearts?* The answer is and always will be love.

My friend Marianne Williamson says, "When we choose to love, or allow our minds to be one with God, then life is peaceful. When we turn away from love, the pain sets in. And whether we love, or close our hearts to love, is a mental choice we make, every moment of every day."[45] We always have a choice to perceive or not perceive love. The choice to open our hearts to love is what feels best, in every situation, every time.

Love is what God is and it is the ultimate reality. The Bible says, "God is love, and whoever abides in love abides in God, and God abides in Him."[46] The feeling of love does not come from us; love is God. As our hearts are open, we allow the love of God to flow through us and out to the world. As we feel loving, we are really feeling the energy of God flowing through us.

Our mission now is to keep our hearts open to this flow of love as much as we possibly can. To do this, we must notice when our hearts have closed. In those moments, we have temporarily "Edged God Out" with E.G.O. thinking. All that is required is to open our minds and hearts to the love of God again.

Keeping our hearts open when someone disappoints or hurts us is not easy. But we wouldn't want it to be easy. Games that are too easy are boring. Learning how to keep our hearts open to the love of God, even during the most challenging moments, is a lifelong quest that will keep us growing and striving until our very last day. That's a worthwhile endeavor. There is no higher calling or path than dedicating our lives to choosing love.

Choose Love First, or Second

When I think of someone who embodies love, I think of Jesus. Regardless of your religion or spiritual path, everyone can appreciate the way Jesus loved. His love never discriminated and never excluded. He loved his enemies and his betrayers. Even as he was being tortured and murdered, he prayed to God to forgive his executioners.

That is next-level love; it's incredibly difficult to love and forgive people *as they harm you*. This is why the path of choosing love is a mountain without a top. There is always another level of love to strive for.

To help me remember to love, I sometimes wear a bracelet with the letters H.W.L.F. This stands for *He Would Love First*. It reminds me that Jesus would choose love first in all situations, and it also reminds me that choosing love first is my happiest decision. Unfortunately, I don't always have the wherewithal to choose love first. When I fail to choose love first, there is an alternative that has served me well; I do the next best thing and decide to choose love second.

On the night of the fireworks, as I was putting our children to bed, I finally recognized that I had failed to choose love first with Katie. I noticed my lack of love was creating a world of suffering for everyone. I decided I would choose love second. The only problem was that I was so far removed from love that I couldn't just snap out of it.

Sometimes, closing your heart can give you too much momentum, and it can be hard to come back. If you are not careful, you can get lost in this dark condition for days, and sometimes, even longer. When I finally recognized my cold-hearted state, I took drastic measures to open my heart again. With my eyes closed, I meditated on Katie's death. I visualized a future with Katie dying in a car crash. I pictured myself at the hospital, getting the news from the doctors that she didn't make it. I saw our children putting roses on her casket as they lowered her into the ground.

I then imagined our lives without her in it; me cooking meals for the children by myself. The melancholy and sad looks on our faces. Tight hugs from my girls as they told me they wished Mommy were here. The life I saw brought me to tears. Contemplating losing a dear loved one can open your heart in a way few other things can. You realize that your petty fights are so unimportant, and you finally recognize that nothing but love matters to you.

When I opened my eyes and brought myself back to the present on that Fourth of July night, my heart was wide open again. With so much love and happiness, I realized my beloved wife was still alive. I asked myself how I would treat her if this were indeed one of the last nights we ever had together. With tears in my eyes, I went to Katie and gave her the biggest hug. I didn't care if she felt cold toward me. I wanted to love her in whatever mood she was experiencing. We fell asleep that night holding hands, open-hearted again.

The best thing you can do is make a conscious decision to choose love first. If you fail, and you will, just pick yourself back up and choose love second. Apologize sincerely and open your heart. It's the only choice that makes sense. As Marianne Williamson said, "We are not held back by the love we didn't receive in the past, but by the love we're not extending in the present."[47]

Choosing Unconditional Love

Love is easy when others are kind, respectful, and thoughtful. It gets much harder when others act in harsh and careless ways. Choosing love regardless of how others act is called unconditional love. This is the way God loves us and how we can strive to love others.

When I was a child, my mother was the purest example of unconditional love. She would tell me that she'd love me no matter what. I would ask her if she would love me even if I failed out of school. She would say that she would love me no matter how I performed. I would ask her if she would love me even if I robbed a bank. She said she would be disappointed, but she would visit me in jail and love me just the same.

I've adopted unconditional love with Katie and my children. I tell them often that no matter what they do or don't do, I will always love them. Sometimes, like the night of the fireworks, I don't choose love first, but I can always find my way back to love rather quickly with them.

Where unconditional love gets harder is when it comes to loving strangers, coworkers, and extended family members who treat us with cruelty. While I have not mastered this level of unconditional love, it is something I strive for. The reason you should strive for unconditional love for all is because the feeling of love is what feels best for you. You are the biggest benefactor of the love you give. The more you choose love, the more happiness you experience. When you choose to love unconditionally, you get to remain unconditionally happy.

When someone is cruel to me, and I have a hard time loving them, I sometimes picture them as a small child. I imagine what their face looked like when they were five. It's easy to love a child who is acting out. Children are so sweet and innocent. Adults acting out are just grown children who happen to be throwing a temper tantrum. Just because someone is now bigger and has hair on their bodies doesn't mean they are mature. An adult who is throwing a tantrum is like a big child who is seeking attention. When you have difficulty choosing love with someone, try picturing what they looked like as a little kid. You might find it easier to extend your compassion and care toward them.

I've found that all actions are typically one of two things: a loving gesture or a cry out for love. When someone is crying out for love, give them your love. You will be the one who benefits the most.

Receiving Love

It can sometimes be easier for us to give love than to receive it. This has certainly been the case for me. I have sometimes felt uncomfortable when others shower me with praise and compliments. I've found myself thinking of ways to compliment them back before they even finish saying their compliment to me. But, being uncomfortable receiving praise and love from others blocks us from becoming our most loving selves.

> We can only give love to the extent that we can receive it.

Often, our biggest barrier to becoming more loving is accepting the fact that we are fully loved and lovable as we are. We deflect praise and compliments because we know that excessive pride is unhealthy, and that humility is the path to good moods. But humility doesn't mean that you must put yourself down or diminish your internal goodness. My favorite quote on humility comes from C. S. Lewis. He said, "Humility is not thinking less of yourself, it's thinking of yourself less."[48] To be humble does not mean you must deny your soul's greatness. In fact, it's prideful ego-thinking to deny the love of God flowing within you. There is a healthy form of pride that accepts the internal beauty and light of your soul. This isn't arrogant or boastful; it's just an honest acceptance of the light of God shining through you.

When you deny the light of your being, you feed the two most destructive bad moods that exist: shame and guilt. As we have learned, the lie of shame is that you are unlovable the way you are, and the lie of guilt is that you don't deserve love because of bad things you have done in your past. If you deflect the love and compliments others show you, you reinforce the lies of shame and guilt within your subconscious. This in turn will have you believing lies about others that they are unlovable and flawed as they are, and that they too deserve punishment for the bad things they have done.

To become more loving toward others, begin to fully receive the love and compliments others give to you. When someone offers you a sincere compliment, as awkward as it may seem at first, stay still and receive it. Don't try to immediately compliment back. Feel the goodness of the love they are giving you. Then, say a sincere and heartfelt, "Thank you." No other words are required. The full acceptance of love for being exactly as you are is your only job in that moment. As you grow in your ability to receive love, you will grow into a more loving person.

Feeling love in your heart never gets old. The more you love, the happier you are. In my podcast interview with Marianne Williamson, she said, "God is love. We are creations of God (meaning we are love too). Our purpose on this Earth is to love. That is when we're happy."[49] When you open your heart, the energy of God's love flows through you, and you are happy. When you close your heart to God's love, you suffer. For this reason, any choice that is not love is a poor choice.

And while this is so much easier said than done, loving yourself and everyone wholeheartedly is a worthwhile pursuit.

The Lie Keeping Us from Love: *I don't feel like being loving.*
The Truth: *It always feels best to be loving. If I ever find my heart closed, I can always choose love again and bring my heart back to happiness.*

CHAPTER 15

Choosing Joy

The Lie Keeping Us from Joy: *I have a valid reason not to love this moment exactly as it is.*

When we think of being in a good mood, we typically picture ourselves with a big smile on our face, feeling happy and lighthearted. What we experience in this moment is the feeling of joy, and it is our natural state of being. If we are ever not experiencing joy, it is because we are blocking it in some way.

To help create more joy in our lives, it is important to understand the difference between joy and pleasure. Pleasure is often a short-lived feeling that comes from external stimuli. It typically fades once the stimulation or object is removed. Eating ice cream, watching our favorite TV show, or shopping can induce feelings of pleasure. While these things can feel nice in the moment, they don't create lasting happiness.

In contrast, joy is a deeper, more fulfilling emotion. It can endure beyond the immediate moment, and we can even experience it while facing challenging circumstances. Unlike pleasure, joy is not dependent on the external situation. Joy comes from within, and it is expressed any time we remove all blocks and barriers to its natural expression. We block the natural flow of joy whenever we are dissatisfied with some aspect of reality.

To understand how joy works, take a moment to think back on times in your life when you felt particularly joyful. Maybe it was your first kiss, or the day your child was born. Perhaps it was the day you won the competition, or you got the big promotion. In those moments when you had an extraordinary life accomplishment, the external world exceeded your expectations. You were not dissatisfied with reality; rather, you were ecstatic with the way your life was unfolding.

You feel joyful whenever you are in love with reality. But joy doesn't need to be limited to only those rare occasions when everything goes better than expected. Joy is an internal choice. While favorable life conditions can certainly help you access joy, the true source of joy comes from your choice to love your life exactly as it is.

Loving What Is

You experience joy when you are in love with the conditions of your life exactly as they are. This is why the day you had your first kiss or won the big match were such joyful days. You weren't dampening your joy with thoughts that your current reality wasn't good enough.

What would happen if you chose to be excited with your life exactly as it was every day? You would feel incredible joy every day.

This is much easier to do when your life is absent of challenges. It's much harder to do when these occur. A while ago I was facing a challenge, and I was blocking my joy by resisting reality. I had just been served a lawsuit as part of a class-action case against realtors. The result of the suit was a court order that reduced the income of our company by a substantial amount. To keep the company open, I had to let good people go. With this lawsuit, I didn't know if I wanted to continue to operate the company at all. So, I began to formulate plans to diversify our income.

I attended a conference about property management and invested in ways to grow our property management division. I made plans to create a coaching program for people looking to achieve Conscious Happiness. I also hired a firm to help me identify and purchase a profitable insurance company.

Even while I was creating these new ventures, I wasn't feeling joyful. I was resisting the changes that I felt had been forced upon me. That is until everything changed on a single phone call. I was talking with the top executive at our real estate firm, Lisa Quick. On the call, Lisa recommended that we embrace the changes to the industry and that we view them as an opportunity. In a single decision, I moved up *The Progression of Moods* from negativity about reality to the good mood of acceptance of our reality.

The next morning, I progressed myself from acceptance to the good mood of gratitude by writing down all the ways I was grateful the lawsuit had happened. I was grateful the suit prompted me to invest in new business ventures and to start a Conscious Happiness coaching program. I wouldn't have taken these positive actions if the lawsuit had not occurred.

From gratitude, I moved myself to love. I decided to embrace the challenge of navigating people I loved through a difficult situation in their real estate careers. After a month of joyless resistance to the change, the joy came back the moment I made the decision to stop being dissatisfied with my reality and chose to embrace it instead.

This is how joy works. As you resist any aspect of your life, you stifle your joy. In the moments of change and hardship, you have every right to feel dissatisfied and upset. But a loss is only a loss so long as you allow it to be so in your mind. At any moment, you are free to reframe the loss into learning, or better yet, into a gain. As soon as you choose to accept reality, to feel grateful for it, and to love it exactly as it is, your joy will return. Joy is not dependent on the external conditions being favorable or unfavorable. It is your natural state of being, and it can be accessed the moment you stop resisting life and choose to love your life, challenges and all.

Joy is a choice.

Sacrificing Joy Is Not Required

Sometimes we limit our joy because we believe in the illusion of sacrifice. On the surface, sacrifice appears to be a noble endeavor. We celebrate people who sacrifice themselves for the greater good. This can lead us to believe that we must sacrifice our joy as well. The truth is that sacrificing our joy is not required.

One of my favorite authors is the late Vietnamese monk, Thich Nhat Hahn. In his book *Peace Is Every Step*, he says, "In the West, we are very goal oriented. We know where we want to go, and we are very directed in getting there. This may be useful, but often we forget to enjoy ourselves along the route."[50] I resonate strongly with this quote. I often put unnecessary pressure on myself to get things done and sacrifice my joy while doing it. I'll toil away doing work I don't like to earn a living. I'll torture myself in a workout to increase my fitness. I'll sacrifice my joy at home to dutifully take care of my family obligations.

If we're not careful, we can find that our whole life has become one big sacrifice. We may achieve success with this approach, but success without joy is the ultimate failure. As Thich Nhat Hanh says, "If we do not have peace and joy right now when will we have peace and joy—tomorrow, or after tomorrow? What is preventing us from being happy right now?"[51] We choose to be happy right now when we set down the illusion that we must sacrifice our joy.

I learned this lesson one Sunday morning. I was having the best day; I had just played basketball with my friends and was heading home for a big family breakfast of blueberry pancakes. That's when I saw the voicemail. It was Kayla, a client of our real estate firm, and she was not happy. An agent from my team was not performing and now he was avoiding her calls. She was furious and her frustration was obvious in the tone of her voicemail.

As I pulled into my driveway, I saw the happiness of my young family through the window as they prepared the pancakes. But I felt obligated to deal with this issue. If I could just sacrifice my joy briefly and knock out this phone call, I could then go inside and have joy with my family.

The ego gives you many compelling reasons why you must sacrifice your joy. It tells you that you really don't have a choice. In this instance, the ego was telling me that if I didn't call Kayla right away, her fury would grow. Then, she might go online and write a terrible review about our company. The ego convinced me that I could sacrifice my joy for a measly ten minutes and then get back to having fun.

On the call, I put on a fake smile and said all the right things. I listened to her upset feelings and validated them. I took responsibility and came up with solutions to make it right for her. She left the call feeling appreciated, while I left feeling drained. After the call, I slouched into my home and set my bags down. The breakfast was less joyful that morning because of my choice to give into the ego's pressure.

When you notice a feeling of obligation, that's your clue that you are believing the ego-lie that you must sacrifice. The ego promises if you just sacrifice your joy in this moment, that it will give you joy in the future. But you cannot experience joy in the future, because the future exists only in your mind. As Thich Nhat Hanh said, "People sacrifice the present for the future. But life is available only in the present."[52]

Don't sacrifice your present joy for the promise of future joy. You can choose to have both joy in the now and joy in the future, too.

You Always Have Options

To break the ego's spell of sacrifice, recognize that you have other options. The ego tries to convince you that you have no other choice, but you always have choices. That Sunday morning with Kayla, the ego pressured me into calling her back right away. It reasoned that I could either suffer through the call now or suffer through it later, but either way, I would suffer. I figured if I was going to suffer either way, I might as well just get it over with. None of this was true. I did not have to suffer. I had other options.

One choice was to never call Kayla back. I could have ghosted her like my agent was doing and blocked her number. That choice would have had consequences, but it was an option. Recognizing you have a choice to not act at all in the moment you feel obligated to act is how you reclaim your power from the ego. For example, if you feel obligated to go to work but don't feel like going, recognize you have a choice to stay home. Sure, there will be consequences for missing work, but you do have a choice.

This is a crucial step to choosing joy, and it's easy to skip over it. When you feel the ego pressure of obligation to sacrifice, take a moment to still yourself until you see that not acting at all is just as valid of an option as acting on the ego's demands. Only once you know that you have the option to not act at all can you ask yourself the next question which is, *"Which choice feels the most joyful to me today?"*

Sometimes, the more joyful choice is to take the vacation day and skip work. Other times, you choose to go to work. But when you choose to do something rather than feel pressured to do it, you can choose to do it with joy. When it's your choice, and not ego pressure or obligation, it feels better because it's on your terms. You chose it. The final step to end the illusion of suffering in sacrifice is to ask yourself the question, *"How could I do this task, and enjoy the process?"*

If I had asked myself that question with Kayla, I could have come up with many creative solutions. Perhaps I could have gone inside, kissed my wife and kids, and asked their permission to call a client before we ate. Or, I could have sent Kayla a text message and said, "I'm so sorry you are upset. I never want you to feel that way. I have a breakfast commitment to attend to right now. I'll call you at noon, and we'll come up with solutions." By the time noon came around, I would have been mentally prepared for the call and most likely enjoyed the conversation because it was on my terms.

When you're faced with an obligation you feel you must do joylessly, don't act until you fully see that you have a choice to never complete the task. Then, if you choose to do it, ask yourself how you could do it and enjoy the process at the same time.

Don't Make the Present Moment a Means to an End

Sometimes we find ourselves sacrificing our joy, even during pleasant experiences. We can get so used to living in our minds, thinking about what is next, that we can no longer enjoy what is happening right now. This is called turning the present moment into a means to an end.

My family had an experience with this a little while ago. My wife and I took our three daughters to a fancy restaurant as a special treat. They were so excited. My wife wanted to make the preparation for the night special. She decided she would create a "spa day" at the house, helping our girls get dressed, putting on their makeup, and doing their hair for the big night. The preparation for the event could have been so joyful, but our daughters were just too excited to go that they couldn't fully appreciate the special time with their mom.

When we arrived at the restaurant, I got excited to talk with my daughters about all the delicious options on the menu. I wanted us to all enjoy considering which appetizers we could order, but my daughters couldn't enjoy the fun of picking out appetizers. They just talked about how hungry they were as they impatiently demanded the food to come sooner.

Once the appetizers arrived, and they got some food in their bellies, I thought they would finally relax and enjoy the meal. But their minds quickly went to what was next; they kept asking when the main course would arrive.

When the main course finally came, their minds quickly fixated on dessert. And before they even finished their dessert, they were asking me if they could watch TV when they got home before bedtime.

Throughout the entire incredible evening, my daughters were so caught up in what was next that they couldn't enjoy the joyful experiences we were having. We all do this. Sometimes, we'll be at a fun party and find ourselves wondering when it will be over. Other times, we'll be doing something we really want to do, but constantly check our phone to see if something *even more exciting* is going on. Or we'll be talking with a loved one, and our minds will be racing about all the things going on later that day. We can live our lives sacrificing the enjoyable present moment for what we anticipate could happen next.

Where are we trying to go? There is nowhere to get. We are already here in the present moment which is always the destination of joy. Whenever you rush through the present, you are simply trying to speed up your life to get to the end. Have you ever thought about what happens at the end of your life? Why would you want to hurry up to get there?

My mom always said, "Life is what happens when you are busy making other plans." This is a wise statement from a wise woman. Learning to experience joy means learning to let go of your thoughts of what is next and be present in the joyful now.

Practicing Joy with Meditation

Learning to appreciate the joy of the now is a skill that takes practice. To access the joy of the present moment, you must train your mind to come into the now. This training is called meditation.

If you don't already have a meditation practice, an easy way to start one is by using a guided meditation app. The app I use is called Calm, but there are also guided meditation podcasts you can listen to for free. In just ten minutes a day, you can train your mind to focus on one simple thing in the present, like your breath.

When you train your mind to focus on the present during a short meditation, you will be able to focus on being present later in the day as well. In time, you may find yourself experiencing joy even while doing tasks that had previously seemed menial, like washing the dishes.

Washing the dishes can be very enjoyable when you stop thinking about what you said earlier, or what you are going to do next. You just choose to be present with the dish in your hand, the warm water, and the soapsuds. You realize there is nowhere else to be. There is nothing else to do. The task at hand is the only thing that exists for you when you are fully present. As you shut your brain off for a while, you find joy in the now.

You are in the middle of eternity at this very moment. Eternity isn't some destination you get to at the end of your life; you are here now. You are right where you are supposed to be. The eternal now is the destination and the end. Choose to love the now, and you will find your joy right here in this moment.

The Lie Keeping Us from Joy: *I have a valid reason not to love this moment exactly as it is.*
The Truth: *Choosing not to love the present moment blocks the flow of joy. I can choose to accept the circumstances currently happening, have gratitude for them, and love them exactly as they are. As I do this, joy flows freely.*

CHAPTER 16

Choosing Peace

The Lie Keeping Us from Peace: *Peace is boring.*

When we live a life of peace, it can feel like our life is too good to be true. Everything just works in a harmonious way. We can even start to wonder when the other shoe will drop and bring us back down to reality.

This happened to my wife and me a while ago. Everything in our careers was working well, our finances were covered, we were healthy, and our relationships were working smoothly. It was heaven on Earth. That is until the other shoe began to drop.

On a perfect evening, I asked Katie if she would be up for a family movie night. She agreed and I gathered the kids and made some popcorn. The children and I got everything set up and picked out a movie we thought Katie would like. Then, we waited for Katie to come sit down with us.

She wasn't coming so we called for her. She said she would be there in just a minute. We waited some more, and everyone began to get antsy. What could be taking her so long? I finally got up from my seat and went back to the bedroom to ask her what was going on. She replied, "I'm busy, start the movie without me."

That's when I started to get frustrated. The movie I picked out was a romantic comedy specifically because I thought Katie would enjoy it. What could be so important that she would skip spending time with us? Trying to keep my cool, I asked her, "What are you working on?"

She said, "I'm trying to get the hot tub phone application fixed. It's acting up."

That's when I lost my cool. Why would she need to fix the hot tub phone app at this exact moment? I said, "Babe, you don't need to work on that right now. We aren't even going to be using the hot tub this weekend. Can you just come watch the movie?"

She shot back, "This has been bothering me and I just want to get it fixed, okay?"

We were about to escalate into a full-fledged fight over nothing. And then, I stopped. I called out what was happening by name as it was happening; we had just hit an *Upper Limits Problem*.

The Upper Limits Problem

Like many of us, I grew up in an emotionally tumultuous household. Things wouldn't stay peaceful for long because our family was addicted to creating drama. As an adult, I continued this trend by manufacturing drama whenever things felt too good.

The reason I was always waiting for the other shoe to drop was because I had an addiction to making it drop. The drama from my childhood felt comfortable to me; it's what I knew. Living in extended periods of peace and happiness was unfamiliar territory. Rather than extend my peace and happiness, I would manufacture drama just to get back to my comfort zone of drama. This is called hitting your *Upper Limit Threshold.*

I learned about the Upper Limit Threshold from psychologist Dr. Gay Hendricks. In *The Big Leap*, he said, "Each of us has an inner thermostat setting that determines how much love, success and creativity we allow ourselves to enjoy. When we exceed our inner thermostat setting, we will often do something to sabotage ourselves, causing us to drop back into the old, familiar zone where we feel secure."[53]

Your Upper Limit thermostat works like the thermostat in your home. If the temperature in your home is set to seventy degrees and the temp rises to seventy-two, the air conditioner kicks on and pushes it back down to seventy. The fight Katie and I were about to co-create over a hot tub and movie night was happening because we had hit the Upper Limit Threshold of peace and happiness in our lives. As Dr. Hendricks describes,

> when you push through your Upper Limit thermostat setting by making more money, experiencing more love, or drawing more positive attention to yourself, you trip your Upper Limit switch. Deep inside your mind a little voice says, "You can't possibly feel this good" (or "make this much money" or "be this happy in love"). Unconsciously you then do something to bring yourself back down to the thermostat setting you're familiar with. Even if you do achieve a glorious new height, it is often short-lived.[54]

Your Upper Limit thermostat was programmed in childhood before you could make decisions for yourself. Usually, your upper limit was mirrored by the amount of peace and happiness the adults in your life allowed themselves to experience. Now, when things get too happy for too long, you will do something to bring your happiness level back down to the "norm" for you.

You most likely don't even notice that you are the one sabotaging your peace. You might get into an "accident," get sick, or have an unexpected conflict in one of your relationships. When you become conscious of this, you may find that most of the drama in your life is subconsciously created by you in response to crossing your Upper Limit Threshold.

Choosing peace is the final stage of *The Progression of Moods* because this is where you learn to allow yourself to experience longer and longer amounts of time in harmony and happiness. Your work at this point is to recognize when your Upper Limit thermostat has been exceeded and to push through the discomfort long enough to adjust your thermostat to a higher setting.

I did this with Katie at the moment we were about to sabotage our peace over a hot tub phone app. I said, "Katie, we have just tripped our Upper Limit thermostat, and we are about to spiral over nothing. I'm totally willing to drop this. I love you. You can work on the hot tub. Just come join us whenever you're ready."

Katie gave me a big hug and the entire fight deescalated immediately. She did choose to fix the hot tub and joined us partway into the movie. We paused the movie and caught her up on what she missed, and we had a lovely evening together. We had just pushed through our previous Upper Limit Threshold and created a new setting for how much peace and happiness we would allow ourselves to enjoy.

How Much Peace Can You Enjoy?

How much peace and happiness can you endure before you feel the urge to spice things up and create a little drama for extra entertainment? Whenever things feel too good to be true, you are feeling that Upper Limit's urge. There is no other shoe that is waiting to drop. Both shoes are securely on your feet and you can choose to keep them there by noticing the urge to create drama and pushing through it.

To the ego, drama is exciting. When there are fires to put out, you get to be the firefighter. This can feel thrilling to the ego. But at this point in your happiness journey, you no longer need to set anything on fire, consciously or subconsciously. A life of peace and happiness is the greatest reward.

People who are addicted to drama may think your new harmonious life is boring. You might eliminate or reduce the amount of alcohol you drink because you notice it adds drama to your choices. You might stop hanging around high-conflict people. You might eliminate high-drama TV programs as you realize you no longer enjoy the anxiety they add to your subconscious mind. You may even stop listening to certain types of music because you realize they are angrier, darker, and more vulgar than your new peaceful thermostat enjoys.

To the rest of the world, your peaceful choices may appear boring. But the rest of the world is run by their egos. Your new life is not boring; it is a sanctuary of harmony, peace, and happiness. To create this life of peace for yourself, there are four major areas of life to focus on: your relationships, your career, your health, and your finances.

Choosing Peace in Your Relationships

Relationships can be the source of the most happiness in our lives. They can also be the source of the most drama. Choosing peace in your relationships starts by choosing peaceful friends. As motivational speaker Jim Rohn famously said, "You are the average of the five people you spend the most time with."[55]

Your brain has mirror neurons, and you naturally mimic the people you spend the most time with. If you want the peace and happiness in your life to improve, choose to spend time with happy and peaceful people. You cannot hang out with high-drama people and expect to have a peaceful life. Some people have a cloud of drama that follows them wherever they go. They constantly gossip, have conflicts in their lives, and find problems around every corner. If you hang around people who create this type of non-peace in their lives, you will find yourself gossiping, complaining, and creating conflict in your life too.

Take a moment to think of the people you hang around most. Grab a pen and write down their names in the "notes" pages at the end of this book. After each name, rate their level of drama on a scale of 1–10. Score people with peace and harmony in their lives lower on this scale, and score people with a lot of drama higher on this scale.

To help facilitate this process, you can download the
Drama-To-Peace-Worksheet at
GoodMoodResources.com

If someone is rated a 7 or higher on your drama scale, you may want to limit their influence in your life. You do this by reaching out to them less, and by reducing the amount of time you get together with them. You don't have to cut anyone out of your life completely if you don't want to. You can still love them and honor the relationship but in a capacity that doesn't harm your peaceful life.

Just know that you are not obligated to spend extended periods of time with anyone who disturbs your harmony, even if they are related to you. As you reduce the time you spend in non-peaceful relationships, you will find space to start new relationships with peaceful people. In time, you will find yourself surrounded by people who respect harmony in their lives and in yours as well.

Choose Peace with Your Finances

The American Psychological Association found that the US has reached a "mental health crisis" based on high levels of stress in the country. They found that the number one contributing factor for stress was financial hardship with forty percent of Americans reporting high or moderate stress from finances.[56] These financial hardships disrupt our peace and reduce our well-being.

According to Financial Health Network, seven out of ten people in America are classified as "financially coping" or "financially vulnerable" compared to just thirty percent who are "financially healthy." This is significant because the vast majority of financially healthy individuals say that their mental well-being is "excellent" or "very good," while less than a quarter of the financially vulnerable individuals report feeling this way.[57]

If you have financial strain, the statistics say that you will struggle to maintain your peace. Thankfully, a man named Dave Ramsey created a *Financial Peace* system that anyone can follow to become financially healthy.[58] Dave Ramsey's method for creating financial peace is simple: Pay off your debts. Dave teaches what he calls the debt snowball.[59] It starts by chopping up your credit cards so you stop using money you don't have. You then reduce your living expenses by cutting out things that are not needed, such as excessive entertainment or luxuries you can do without.

With the money you save on luxuries, you aggressively pay off your smallest debt first while making minimum payments on all other debts. You do this until the smallest debt is fully paid off. This eliminates one payment you used to have, increasing your financial health.

As soon the smallest debt is paid off, you take all the money you were using to pay off that debt, and you pay off the next smallest debt. When the next debt is paid off, you use all your resources and pay off the next smallest debt. You do this until every debt is paid off. This is the path to financial freedom, the ultimate level of financial peace.

Early in our marriage, Katie and I started following Dave Ramsey's financial peace system. We cut up our credit cards and bought everything with cash or debit cards. This forced us to only buy things we could afford.

We started our debt snowball by aggressively paying off my credit card, which was our smallest debt at the time. It took us four months, but we paid it off. When that debt was gone, we used all our resources to attack Katie's credit card. That took us eight months of effort. When it was paid off, we focused on paying off my car loan. A year later, we focused on paying off Katie's car loan. Within three years, we were debt free other than our mortgage payment. Because we had chopped up our credit cards, we also stopped putting ourselves further in debt.

But we didn't stop there. After fourteen years and a great deal of effort, we finally paid off our house. This was the moment we became financially free. None of it would have been possible if we hadn't been introduced to the incredible work of Dave Ramsey.

If you are one of the seventy percent of Americans who are financially coping or financially vulnerable, as Katie and I were, you can become financially healthy if you follow Dave Ramsey's plan. Pay off your debts with a ferocious focus. The research shows that doing this will significantly increase your mental health and peace of mind.

Choose Peace in Your Career

Many times we stay in a career we don't like because we feel trapped and think we need the paychecks to survive. Choosing to work in a career you hate is not the path of a peaceful life. You would have far more peace if you chose a career doing something you love, even if it meant earning less money.

Other times, in our careers, we get into conflicts with others over money. This also robs our peace. Earlier in my career, I would get into conflicts with others about little things. I thought I had to fight for every dollar. Often, the fighting would give me a financial gain but at the cost of my peace.

My wife has taught me a lot about adding peace to my career. She would much rather pay a small sum of money and keep her peace. This doesn't mean that she gives any sum of money to anyone who asks for it. But if the sum of money is small enough, and it doesn't have much of a financial impact on her life, she gladly pays it to buy back her peace. Purchasing your peace is one of the best ways to spend your money. What else do you really want other than peace and happiness? It has taken me years of learning from Katie about this principle. I now realize that if a career problem can be solved with money, and I have the money, then I really don't have a problem.

Perhaps you are in a career you love, but money is the source of your stress. If that's the case, then do as Jim Rohn says and "learn to work harder on yourself than you do on your job. If you work hard on your job, you can make a living, but if you work hard on yourself, you'll make a fortune."[60] As you grow yourself into the person deserving of the paychecks you want, you will attract those paychecks.

You grow yourself and your career by the books you read and the people you meet. Invest in yourself and you will find your investments paying off with bigger paychecks in time. Reading a self-development book for just thirty minutes each day and attending a self-improvement conference a few times each year will be sufficient to help you grow in your career.

Choose Peace in Your Health

To choose peace in your health, choose to honor your body and care for it. This means being mindful of the food you consume and the chemicals you expose yourself to. We all know the things that harm our health. If we overeat, we put unnecessary strain on our system. If we drink, use drugs, or smoke, we harm our minds and bodies. To value peace in your health, choose to eat and drink things that add to the peace and harmony in your mind and body.

A diet that contains high amounts of fruits or vegetables will aid your health. Avoid processed foods and eat whole foods instead. Drink water instead of sugary or caffeinated drinks. Choose to move your body with exercise. Our ancestors used to walk long distances each day to get water. They also lifted firewood on a daily basis and worked hard in the fields to cultivate crops. You choose peace in your health by choosing to walk, lift things, and move your body each day. It's how you are designed. The more energy you expend, the more energy you have.

Getting outside also adds peace to your health. I interviewed one of the world's foremost experts on natural health, Dr. Jack Wolfson, on the *Good Mood Revolution* podcast and he said, "The more time we spend outside, the healthier and happier we are."[61] His best advice to improve our health was to spend time outside each day. You can accomplish this by going for a walk before or after work, or at lunchtime. It's simple advice, and it makes a big difference in the way you feel.

Health problems will inevitably come for all of us, regardless of how healthy we choose to live. None of us are getting out of here alive. But you can find comfort in the inevitable decline of your body by caring for your health the best you can now. This will allow you to face your eventual health problems with your head held high.

Trusting God

The final step on *The Progression of Moods* is to trust God. The entire progression has been a movement from the lowest bad moods of the ego to the highest good moods of the soul. At the top of the progression is God. There ultimately will not be peace until we find the peace of God.

You will never completely rid your life of challenges. To be at peace, you must find comfort as you traverse life's greatest discomforts.

Trusting God is not a step that is taken once; it must be taken daily. We have this illusion that we will get to the point in our lives when we will be free of all problems, and *on that day*, we will finally have peace. But God doesn't want everything to be comfortable for you. If he wanted you to be comfortable, wouldn't you think he had the power to make your life that way?

When life is challenging and uncomfortable, you must trust that God is good and that he is always concerned with your greatest good. He presents you with challenge, not to harm you, but to give you an opportunity to grow into the most loving, compassionate, and humble version of yourself.

God wants you to keep growing, and growth is uncomfortable. If you are still alive, you still have lessons to learn. With this knowledge, drop the illusion that you will get to the point when everything will be comfortable. To live in peace, realize that God has a plan for your growth and for the greater good of your soul's development. Trust that his plan is better than your desire for comfort, and you will find peace as you grow into the greatest expression of yourself.

The Lie Keeping Us from Peace: *Peace is boring.*
The Truth: *Drama does not make life more enjoyable, just more chaotic. I increase my peace by raising my Upper Limits of happiness and by developing a fierce trust in God.*

CONCLUSION

We began this journey seeking happiness. While we are at the conclusion, we are not at the end of your happiness journey—it is just the beginning. The Good Mood Revolution is not just in these pages; it has been unfolding within you. I'm so excited for your future, and for the happiness you will be spreading in the world around you.

As you reflect on your journey, think about *The Progression of Moods* you have ascended. You have successfully learned how to conquer the eight primary bad moods: shame, guilt, hopelessness, sadness, fear, desire, anger, and pride. You have also learned to choose the eight primary good moods: humility, responsibility, confidence, acceptance, gratitude, love, joy, and peace.

If you have not done so already, download the exercises that accompany this book at *GoodMoodResources.com* and come back to them whenever you need.

You now know that your happiness is a conscious choice and not a chance occurrence. You are free to claim it at any time by shifting your perspective.

My hero's journey from bad moods to good is one that is ongoing. I still find myself feeling each of the eight primary bad moods. When I started my quest to find authentic happiness, I wanted to rid myself of all bad moods. I no longer feel this way. I've found that all emotions are here to serve us and help us in some way. The darkness is an essential part of us ... but so is the light.

Now, it's your turn to act on what you've learned. Choose to start each morning with a good mood intention. Perhaps you can start your day by counting your wins and the things you are grateful for. Or listen to the *Good Mood Revolution* podcast and join me each week as we continue to learn how to be our best selves together. Happiness is better with friends. You may even want to share this book with someone you care about.

The blessings in your future are beyond your wildest dreams. Just picture your life without the weight of ego negativity and with the unshakable confidence that comes from living according to your highest virtues. See a future where each challenge is no longer a roadblock but a stepping stone to greater understanding and compassion. As you consistently choose good moods, not only will you be happier, but your light will illuminate the way for others to follow.

Lastly, I want to express my heartfelt appreciation to you, the reader. Thank you for your courage to take this journey through the darkness. You have shown the willingness to choose what is right over what is self-serving. Your reward is a life of conscious happiness.

The Truth: *You are the light.*

ACKNOWLEDGMENTS

I am deeply grateful to God for the guidance, strength, and inspiration provided throughout this journey. Without divine guidance, the *Good Mood Revolution* wouldn't be here.

Thank you to my incredible wife, Katie; your unwavering love, patience, and support have been more appreciated than you will ever know. You have carried more than your share of the load while giving me space to follow the song in my heart. Thank you, my love. I wouldn't want to do any of this without you.

To my wonderful children, Harper, Cameron, Kelly, and Brady: thank you for your boundless love and for bringing joy into our lives every single day.

To my mom, Issy Burch: thank you for being my hero. It was your unconditional love, and the lessons of positivity you instilled in me my whole life that set me on this path.

I want to extend my heartfelt thanks to Tucker Max, Emily Gindlesparger, Hussein Al-Baiaty, and Chas Hoppe at Scribe Media. Thank you for teaching me how to write a book. And to Andrea Cagan: thank you for helping me clear out the clutter and find a structure for this book.

Thank you to my editors Ezra Byer and Katie Smith. Your enthusiasm for this topic, and for helping me see blind spots in my thinking, have been invaluable. Your suggestions have made this book far better than it would have been without you. To Shandi Thompson, Alison Morse, and Adam Witty at Forbes Books: thank you for bringing this project to life in such a big way. To Megan Elger and Erik Cabral: thank you for the work on the logo and the cover. It's beautiful.

To my siblings, friends, teachers, coaches, and mentors. I've learned and grown because of my relationship with each of you. To my friends Marianne Williamson, Dr. Benjamin Hardy, Lou Holtz, and Mark Nepo: thank you for your friendship and guidance along this journey. Each of you has profoundly enhanced my understanding of what it means to live a fulfilling life.

To Dr. David Hawkins, Tony Robbins, Eckhart Tolle, Michael Singer, and to the countless others I have learned and studied from. This book stands on your shoulders and your profound teachings and insights. Also, a big thank you to my coach Steve Gill. Thank you for your coaching and guidance in my life. Steve, you helped me to the other side of so many of the stories in this book, and your words of strength and wisdom still ring in my head as I encounter challenges.

To Mathew Micheletti and Ashley Cottrell: thank you for *The Inner Work*. Mat, your love and support has been the biggest contributor to my emotional growth. Many of the lessons in this book are because you have guided me to these understandings. You are one of the most positive influences in my life and I am forever grateful.

To the people at Matt O'Neill Real Estate and Tide Property Management who have stuck with me through good times and bad. You have helped me understand what it means to have a family at work.

To all the people who have challenged me and forced me to work on my growth and development. In the end, I know that adversaries are just friends in disguise. Thank you for helping me evolve and become more compassionate and understanding.

To all of the guests on the *Good Mood Revolution* podcast. Thank you for bringing your insights to the show and for growing my understanding of what it means to be consciously happy.

Finally, to you, the reader. Thank you for reading this book. It was my burning desire to connect with you and to help you find conscious happiness that compelled me to embark on this work in the first place.

Love,

Matt

AUTHOR BIO

Matt O'Neill is a renowned podcast host, entrepreneur, and devoted family man with a mission to spread positivity. Through the *Good Mood Revolution* podcast, Matt engages with influential thought leaders, offering valuable insights to enhance everyday happiness. As the CEO of Matt O'Neill Real Estate and co-founder of Tide Property Management, his visionary leadership has spurred significant success and growth. His company has been recognized as the number one company to work for in the state of South Carolina by Charleston Business Magazine and listed among the *Inc.* 5000 fastest-growing companies in the nation. Matt resides in Charleston, South Carolina, with his wife, Katie, and their four children. He embraces the belief that life's true purpose is happiness and strives to make this his reality each and every day.

NOTES

NOTES

NOTES

NOTES

NOTES

NOTES

NOTES

ENDNOTES

1   The Dalai Lama and Howard C. Cutler, *The Art of Happiness* (London: Hodder and Stoughton, 1999).

2   Erik H. Erikson, *Childhood and Society* (New York; W.W. Norton and Co., 1950)

3   Eckhart Tolle, *A New Earth: Awakening to Your Life's Purpose* (Penguin Publishing Group, 2006).

4   Mathew Micheletti and Ashley Cottrell (The Yoga Couple), *The Inner Work: An Invitation to True Freedom and Lasting Happiness* (independently published, 2019), 123.

5   Bill Walsh, https://www.azquotes.com/quote/695992.

6   David R. Hawkins, *Letting Go: The Pathway of Surrender* (Veritas Publishing, 2013).

7   Sharon Salzberg, *The Force of Kindness: Change Your Life with Love & Compassion* (Sounds True Publishing, 2010).

8   Angela Duckworth, *Grit: The Power of Passion and Perseverance* (New York: Scribner, 2016).

9   Good Mood Revolution podcast. Empowered Empath with Christa Carpenter https://podcasts.apple.com/us/podcast/empowered-empath-with-krista-carpenter/id1617660263?i=1000585328489 .

10   J. K. Rowling, *Very Good Lives: The Fringe Benefits of Failure and the Importance of Imagination* (Little, Brown and Company, 2015).

11   Post Wire Report, "Catherine Zeta-Jones says there is 'no need to suffer silently,'" NY Post, April 20, 2011, https://nypost.com/2011/04/20/catherine-zeta-jones-says-there-is-no-need-to-suffer-silently/.

12   Thich Nhat Hanh, *The Heart of the Buddha's Teaching* (Harmony, 1999).

13   Good Mood Revolution podcast. Overcoming Fear with #1 Coach Steve Gill. https://podcasts.apple.com/us/podcast/overcoming-fear-with-1-coach-steve-gill/id1617660263?i=1000558601636

14   Amy J. C. Cuddy, Caroline A. Wilmuth, and Dana R. Carney. "The benefit of power posing before a high-stakes social evaluation," Harvard Business School Working Paper, No 13-027, September 2012.

15   Carol S. Dweck, *Mindset: The New Psychology of Success* (New York: Ballantine Books, 2006).

16   Napoleon Hill, *Think and Grow Rich* (Mumbai: Amazing Reads, 2014).

17   Rhonda Byrne, *The Secret* (Atria Books/Beyond Words, 2006).

18   "Success through goal setting, Part 1 of 3," https://www.briantracy.com/blog/personal-success/success-through-goal-setting-part-1-of-3.

19   Good Mood Revolution podcast. Happiness = Progress: Setting Big Goals with Matt King. https://podcasts.apple.com/us/podcast/happiness-progress-setting-big-goals-with-matt-king/id1617660263?i=1000640884951.

20   "Success through goal setting, Part 1 of 3."

21   The Arbinger Institute, *Leadership and Self-Deception: Getting out of the Box* (Berrett-Koehler Publishers, 2015).

22 Nelson Mandela, *Long Walk to Freedom: The Autobiography of Nelson Mandela* (Little, Brown, 2008).

23 Dave Ramsey, *The Total Money Makeover: A Proven Plan for Financial Fitness* (Nashville: Thomas Nelson, 2013).

24 Byron Katie, "Judge your neighbor worksheet," https://thework.com.

25 Byron Katie and Stephen Mitchell, *Loving What Is: Four Questions That Can Change Your Life* (Three Rivers Press, 2003).

26 Ibid.

27 Maya Bell, "Don't let the small stuff get you down," March 22, 2021, University of Miami, https://news.miami.edu/stories/2021/03/dont-let-the-small-stuff-get-you-down.html.

28 Byron Katie, *A Friendly Universe: Sayings to Inspire and Challenge You* (TarcherPerigee, 2013).

29 Byron Katie, "The work," https://thework.com/.

30 David Hawkins, *The Map of Consciousness Explained* (Hay House Inc., 2020), 84–85.

31 David Goggins, *Can't Hurt Me: Master Your Mind and Defy the Odds* (Lioncrest Publishing, 2018).

32 Ibid.

33 Ibid.

34 "Years of Athletic Achievement," davidgoggins.com, accessed July 2, 2024, https://davidgoggins.com/athletic-achievements/.

35 Napoleon Hill, *Think and Grow Rich*.

36 *Good Mood Revolution*, "The new dimension of happiness with Ryan A. Bush," https://podcasts.apple.com/nz/podcast/the-new-dimension-of-happiness-with-ryan-a-bush/id1617660263?i=1000638918055.

37 Jim Collins, *Good to Great: Why Some Companies Make the Leap ... And Others Don't* (Harper Business, 2001).

38 Hal Elrod, Mike McCarthy, and Lindsay McCarthy, T*he Miracle Morning for Parents & Families: How to Bring Out the Best in Your Kids and Your Self* (Hal Elrod International, Inc., 2016).

39 Martin E. P. Seligman and Christopher Peterson, *Character Strengths and Virtues: A Handbook and Classification* (Oxford: Oxford University Press, 2004).

40 "Jane Goodall," https://www.britannica.com/biography/Jane-Goodall.

41 Jeffrey Sanzel, "Movie Review: New Nat Geo documentary on Jane Goodall gives the world hope," May 15, 2020, https://tbrnewsmedia.com/movie-review-new-nat-geo-documentary-on-jane-goodall-gives-the-world-hope/.

42 "Jane Goodall," https://education.nationalgeographic.org/resource/jane-goodall/.

43 Darren Hardy, *The Compound Effect* (Bhopal: Manjul Publishing House, 2021).

44 Steve Jobs, "Stanford commencement speech," June 12, 2005, https://news.stanford.edu/2005/06/12/youve-got-find-love-jobs-says/.

45 Marianne Williamson, *A Return to Love* (HarperOne, 1996).

46 1 John 4:16.

47 Marianne Williamson, *A Return to Love*.

48 Nathan Dean, "C.S. Lewis on humility," September 7, 2018, https://onechristianlife.com/c-s-lewis-on-humility/.

49 Good Mood Revolution Podcast. A Return to Love with Marianne Williamson https://podcasts.apple.com/us/podcast/a-return-to-love-with-marianne-williamson/id1617660263?i=1000589877187.

50 Thich Nhat Hanh, *Peace Is Every Step: The Path of Mindfulness in Everyday Life* (Random House Publishing Group, 1992).

51 Ibid.

52 Ibid.

53 Gay Hendricks, *The Big Leap: Conquer Your Hidden Fear and Take Life to the Next Level* (HarperOne, 2010).

54 Ibid.

55 Jim Rohn quotes, https://www.goodreads.com/quotes/1798-you-are-the-average-of-the-five-people-you-spend.

56 APA, "Stress in America™ 2020," https://www.apa.org/news/press/releases/stress/2020/report-october.

57 Financial Health Network, "Understanding the mental-financial health connection," https://finhealthnetwork.org/research/understanding-the-mental-financial-health-connection/.

58 Dave Ramsey, *The Total Money Makeover* (Thomas Nelson, 2013).

59 Ibid.

60 Jim Rohn quotes, https://www.goodreads.com/quotes/7898460-learn-to-work-harder-on-yourself-than-you-do-on.

61   Good Mood Revolution Podcast. Great Health Awakening: Millions Sick, One Simple Solution with Dr. Jack Wolfson https://podcasts.apple.com/us/podcast/great-health-awakening-millions-sick-one-simple-solution/id1617660263?i=1000640219198

Printed in the USA
CPSIA information can be obtained
at www.ICGtesting.com
JSHW022153041224
74790JS00001B/14